THE BEAUTY OF

MAKKAH
&
MADINAH

MOHAMED AMIN

First published 1999 by
Camerapix Publishers International Ltd,
PO Box 45048,
Nairobi,
Kenya.

This book was designed and produced by
Camerapix Publishers International Ltd.

Production Director: Rukhsana Haq
Editors: Jan Hemsing
Research: Zulf M Khalfan
Design: Shameer Shah
Production Assistant: Rachel Musyimi

ISBN 1 874041 53 9

Printed in Singapore by Tien Wah Press

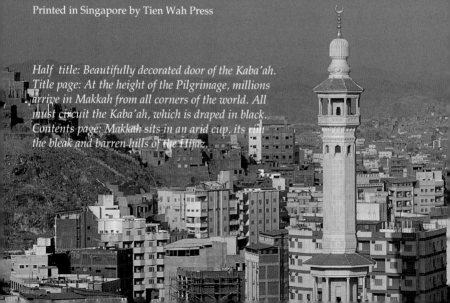

Half title: Beautifully decorated door of the Kaba'ah.
Title page: At the height of the Pilgrimage, millions
arrive in Makkah from all corners of the world. All
must circuit the Kaba'ah, which is draped in black.
Contents page: Makkah sits in an arid cup, its rim
the bleak and barren hills of the Hijaz.

CONTENTS

*And proclaim unto
mankind the Pilgrimage.
They will come unto
thee on foot and
on every lean camel;
they will come from
every deep ravine*
Qur'an XXII - 27

Above: Detail of a page from the early Qur'an.

Introduction

Makkah, the focal point of the Islamic faith, stirs the imagination as few other places in the world. Forbidden to all but Muslims, yet known and talked about by all the world's people, Makkah is a 59-kilometre-long sanctuary with a permanent population of more than 600,000. This swells to almost three million during the Pilgrimage — known as the Hajj — when pilgrims from all over the world flock to the city to fulfil one of the five pillars of Islam.

The beauty of Makkah and Madinah and their spiritual integrity and mysticism have made the sanctuary one of the religious centres of the world.

The impact of the Prophet Muhammad, the birth of Islam in Makkah, and their shared destiny, are reflected in the light of the special status given to the city in the Holy Qur'an.

This book gives, for the first time, a detailed step-by-step explanation of each ceremony of the Hajj and Umrah and also serves as a useful guide to all Muslims, especially prospective pilgrims, and to non-Muslims with a general interest, who cannot go to Makkah.

1. The Arabian Peninsula: Early History

In the west of Arabia, desolate, barren but ruggedly beautiful, lies a 1,400-kilometre-long ridge of mountains, a natural fortification known as "The Barrier" — the Hijaz. Inhabited years ago by Bedouin nomads, who formed four-fifths of its mainly pagan population, a system of spiritual thought adulterated with idolatry prevailed in the peninsula, along with widely held traditional values. Among these, hospitality was most highly ranked. Endowed with absolute individual liberty, the Bedouins nonetheless were subject to the vagaries of fate. A sudden drought, an unpredictable disaster, disease or famine were all events which left them dependent for survival on the good will of total strangers. Thus, logic indicated that, in good times, an unexpected guest or the arrival of a stranger called for an unlimited welcome. Bounty was heaped upon them in the form of food, drink, festivity and shelter — for who could tell when such kindness might be required from the guests in return?

The Bedouin environment created a scale of masculine virtues without equal. Many qualities were admired. *Murrwah* — "what fits a man" — had many values, of which one was the absolute respect given to women. They enjoyed considerable independence in these nomadic societies, and were required to give shelter to their husbands whenever needed, rather than take up residence with them. It was a loosely bound society, interwoven with a network of clan systems which occasionally erupted in feuding over grazing rights or political squabbles. Now *Hijaz* has come to be used as a general term for the people and area of Makkah.

Surrounded by powerful neighbours — the Byzantine Empire in the north-west, Persia to the north-east and Ethiopia in Africa across the straits of Mandab — the Bedouins had plenty of distractions to fuel their political disunity.

Quarrels over water, pasture and trade routes compounded their differences. Instead of serving as a unifying factor, the Arabic language helped only to articulate parochial and tribal differences and divergencies. There was no central government in those early days. Each tribe was a law unto itself and the Hijaz was preserved from foreign domination. One lone factor, however, held the Bedouins of the Barrier together — the constant attraction of the *Kaba'ah*, the holy shrine centred in Makkah, to which all paid homage even in those pre-Islamic days.

Makkah Before Islam

Long before the advent of Islam, Makkah had its own status as an historical centre, albeit a minor one. Ptolemy, the Egyptian geographer, called it "Macoraba". The city stands in a dusty depression ringed by desert mountains. From time immemorial, it has sheltered the Kaba'ah, a simple, cube-shaped stone edifice which was built by Ibrahim and his son, Ismael.

The valley, conveniently placed at the extreme ends of Asia and Africa, near a gap in the Sarat range of mountains, is on the road from Babylonia and Syria to the plateau of the Yemen on the shores of the Red Sea. The latter enabled it to communicate with the African continent long before the western world did.

Situated at the crossroads of two major caravan routes, Makkah was an established station on "the incense route" through which expensive perfumes, spices and silks from the East reached the Mediterranean — a route which led from Central Asia and Iran through Makkah to the Mediterranean basin. The other trading route crossed from central Asia and Iran through the Arabian steppe to Africa. Thus, from the earliest times, Makkah's location made it an important commercial centre. The valley cradling the Kaba'ah had one resource which gave it permanency — a well, known as *Zamzam*, which provided a regular if variable source of water.

In their early period, Makkans engaged in political and commercial deals with neighbouring Arabian states, giving safe conduct to traders and free passage of their caravans, referred to by historians as the "guarantee of Caesar and Chosroes". The most influential of these early traders were chiefs of the tribe known as Quraysh. They made agreements with the Negus of Abyssinia, the Sheikhs of Najd, the Kails of Yemen and the Phylarchs of Ghassan and Hira.

Negotiations with the Greeks and Persians were conducted at trading posts on the frontier or in specially designated towns. In Palestine, these

Previous pages: North-east of Makkah is Mount Hira, where an angel commanded Muhammad to be God's messenger.

were the ports of Aila and Ghazza, and probably the town of Jerusalem. In Syria, Basra was the main market. Despite many restrictions, the Quraysh chiefs managed to obtain trade permits as a result of these negotiations. Eastern governments forbade free trade because they generally distrusted merchants. Byzantium was ever-suspicious of foreigners, especially Bedouins who, as a consequence, were heavily taxed and often had to hand over "hostages" before negotiations began.

In retaliation, Makkah levied charges on foreign traders in the form of tithes, entry and travel visas, trading permits, departures and export taxes, a number of which required guarantees from the local clan or one of its notable members.

Makkans claimed descent from a common ancestor of humble origin, a man called Quraysh, who lived in the mountains above Makkah. But there were forcible introductions — some 10 main clans from the northern end of the Hijaz were probably installed by the Qusaily when they conquered the area occupied by the Khuza'ah tribe and settled in the centre of the town, near the Kaba'ah, where the water from the Zamzam well accumulated.

Thus, this central quarter came to be identified with the aristocracy, and was where the oldest Quraysh families lived. Other clans lived on the outskirts of the town and others, more distant from the Quraysh, dwelt on the mountain slopes overlooking the city, earning them the name "the Quraysh of the outskirts". They were considered braver soldiers than those Makkans "of the centre".

In pre-Islamic Makkah, there were no officials to administer taxes, though tradition has recorded a number of "honorary offices" without jurisdiction. The chiefs constituted a regular official body, a kind of Grand Council — *dar al nadwah* — which met periodically. Decisions on matters of general interest, however, were taken in the *majlis*, the family groups, or in the *nadi gawm*, the town forum in the square of the Kaba'ah. The early town occupied the bottom of the *wadi*, or the valley, more commonly known as the *batn Makkah*, the hollow of Makkah or *al-Batha*. A cluster of buildings in this quarter were so close to the Kaba'ah that their shadows merged with each other. An open area between the Kaba'ah and their buildings formed the primitive *Masjid*, a sanctuary

Above: The highway running into the hills past Mount Hira leads to the Plain of Arafat.

Above: A figure-of-eight flyover and modern road network on the outskirts of Makkah, designed exclusively for the Pilgrimage.

open to the heavens. There was little else in pre-Islamic Batha.

The streets from the houses which led to this area were called "the gates of the *Haram* or the Masjid" and took their names from the respective clans who settled around the Kaba'ah. The chief families met on the ground floor of the buildings facing the side of the Kaba'ah. Conditions in the suburbs were sub-standard, described by two historians as "a confusion of poor houses, low and ramshackle hovels". Shortage of water was the main problem, because the output of the Zamzam was variable.

Rains are rare, with drought often lasting up to four years, making the residents dread *Ramda Makkah*, "the burning heat of Makkah", which forces some families to send their children to the cooler regions. But when the rains finally come, they do so as violent torrents, causing damage in the hollow area, which inevitably becomes flooded. In the past, before adequate measures were taken to thwart floods from the rain-waters, heavy downpours damaged the Kaba'ah, creating temporary lakes in the area where it was situated. The sterile Makkah soil also often threatened famine when grain convoys from Syria were delayed.

An active mercantile atmosphere prevailed in Makkah. Writing and arithmetic played an important part in the town. However, except for 15 Quraysh individuals identified by historians, most of the families in pre-Islamic Makkah were illiterate. Scales and crude records of accounts were prominent in Makkah shops, mostly to verify payments. Professional weighers, *wazzan*, were available to resolve disputes. Coins, which were scarce, were supplemented by precious metal, such as ingots of gold or silver, and by *tibr*, or gold dust. Later, the *denarius aureus* of the Byzantines and the silver drachm of the Sasanids and Himyar reached Makkah. These coins, of varied crude engravings and unequal weight, caused confusion in the market. Only the expert money-changer with a careful eye could determine their true values.

Capital circulated freely in the Makkah society, while the businessman, *tajir*, hoarded his, accumulating wealth in strong boxes. Brokers and agents thrived, as most of the population lived on credit. Sleeping partnerships — *mudaraba* — on the basis of 50 per cent profit participation were greatly favoured. This state of commerce enabled even the poor to

invest their gold *dinar* or half-*dinar* in a business enterprise, a *nashsh*. Differences in standards complicated exchange transactions. The Byzantine provinces of Syria and Egypt were on the gold standard, the *ahl-dhahab*, while Babylonia was on the Sasanian silver standard, the *ahl al-warik*. Money was the principal item of transaction of the Makkah businessman. Occasionally, he would invest his money in another business, such as the organisation of a large caravan. Makkah was mainly a banking town or clearing-house. Interest at 100 per cent was prevalent and speculation was high on loads of caravans, flocks of livestock and provisions for the town. Fictitious associations were formed to loan money for sales and purchases. As the *hadith* states: "He who was not a merchant counted for nothing." Women engaged actively in business enterprise and are said to have participated in tribal combat. Among the prominent businesswomen of Makkah was Khadijah, daughter of Khuwaylid, who became the first wife of the Prophet. She engaged in foreign trade, playing an important part in His material advancement during His younger days.

Two of the wives of the companions of the Prophet were commercially minded: Abu Jahl's mother operated a perfumery, while Hind, Abu Sufyan's wife, sold her merchandise to the Kalbis of Syria.

Despite their wealth, probably because they were people of the desert, Makkans did not own ships. Foreign ships anchored in the small off-desert bay of Shuaiba, where the wreck of a Byzantine ship lay. The timbers of its wood went into the building of the Kaba'ah. The near shore of Jeddah was desolate.

Left: The huge Mosque with its slender minarets dominates its surroundings.

2. Historic Makkah

Makkah became more important after the birth of the Prophet Muhammad and the advent of Islam, *circa* 570CE, the city being so strongly linked with the birth of the new religion of Islam and its Prophet. *(According to the Qur'an, Islam is not a new religion, but is the very first and the only true religion prescribed by God through a long chain of Prophets, beginning with Adam and ending in Muhammad. Some of the other links in the chain are Abraham, Moses and Jesus Christ.)* Despite its sunken location, secured by stolid surrounding hills, Makkah claims a pivotal role in Islam's destiny. The Qur'an, itself the final revealed scriptures given by God to introduce mankind to a timeless and complete way of life and to unfold its sacred tenets, gave concrete legitimacy to Muhammad as the true and final Prophet of Allah, and accords this once remote city the supreme title of *"umm al-qura"* — "the mother of cities".

It has also been known as *"bait al-atiq"*, "the Ancient House", and *"Baytullah"*, "the House of God". The Makkan territory has been described as the core of the earth, while the central depression of the valley, where the city nestles, has been dubbed "the navel" of the world.

There is no doubt that the dawn of Islam rescued Makkah from the "Age of Ignorance", thrusting it into a period of enlightened growth to give it a unique role in the dynamic expansion of Islam, which today claims more than 900 million followers.

The Struggle: Prophet Muhammad and Makkah: 612-632CE

The Prophet Muhammad (bin'Abd Allah bin'Abd al-Muttalib) was born in Makkah in the care of a well-placed Hashemite family who were guardians of the Kaba'ah. Although illiterate, when He was about 42 years old, in 612CE, He received the divine revelations of the Holy Qur'an on Mount Hira, an event which put Him and Makkah on a common course with the spread of Islam. At first, because of His attacks on idol worship in Makkah and His preaching, which criticised material possession while encouraging honesty, courtesy, charity and respect for women, the Prophet was viewed with great suspicion by the Makkans.

Makkan tradesmen ignored His teaching against paganism, polytheism and worship of deities — *al-Lat*, *al-Uzza* and *Manat* — and

later came to regard Him as a threat to their trade. Though He treated them with great courtesy, He, His wife, close members of the family and His early followers were mocked and abused. They endured numerous persecutions, which increased so much that in 622CE, the epochal year of the Islamic Calendar, they migrated to Madinah. This important event is known as the *Hijrah*. This period marked the beginning of an intense campaign against the 'Muslims' by the Makkans. During this period, the Prophet went on a divine mission to Taif, a vineyard town in the hills, where He was pelted with stones. He had to return to Makkah, in pain and anguish. Nevertheless, He was gaining new adherents from far and wide in Arabia, although few in number. In 622CE, He took an oath of allegiance from a group of Muslims from Madinah after a similar meeting the previous year with pilgrims from Madinah in al-Akaba. They pledged to accept Him as a citizen of Madinah and protect Him and His followers. In the second year of the Hijrah, 624CE, an outnumbered force of Muslims defeated Makkan forces led by Abu Sufyan, at the famous battle of Badr. Abu Jahl was killed, while the Prophet's uncle, Abbas, and others were taken prisoner.

In 628CE, the Treaty of Hudaybiya granted the Prophet Muhammad permission to make the *Hajj*, or Pilgrimage, the following year. In 630CE, Makkah surrendered peacefully to Muslims. When, two years later, in 632CE, the Prophet died, Saidna Abu Bakr, one of Muhammad's most able companions, was acclaimed Caliph and the new leader of the Islamic community and state. It was he who collected the Qur'an into one volume before his death in 634CE. He was succeeded by Umar, a grandson of the Prophet, and during Umar's reign, Egypt, Syria and Persia were conquered. When Umar died, he was succeeded by another grandson, Usman, who invaded Cyprus. Upon Usman's death in 655CE, the Prophet's son-in-law, Ali, became Caliph.

There is no true way to measure Muhammad's contribution. Through the revelation of the Qur'an, the Prophet gave the Makkans a *raison d'etre* and, through the teachings of Islam, a new sense of identity. His long-term impact on the city and its social, cultural and economic character defies assessment. His unique and imposing personality and exemplary life, based on divine inspiration, gave rise to timeless legends and

Left: A wall at the foot of the Mount of Mercy commemorates the spirit of Islam.

Below: A pilgrim from India clasps his hands in prayer atop the Mount of Mercy.

Above: Bab-al Umra, the second main entrance situated in the south-west of the Grand Mosque.

traditions, collected by His followers in the hadith, which not only revived and nourished the spiritual and social life of Makkah but spilled beyond its boundaries, across the mirages of the Hijaz desert, to merge with hitherto unimagined cultures.

The establishment of the Islamic State in Madinah by the Prophet inevitably affected the economic prosperity of Makkah. Under the first three Caliphs, many families migrated to Madinah. Moreover, other men from Makkah were given various posts in different provinces of the rapidly expanding Islamic realm. In the fervent years of rapid Islamic growth, shortly after the death of the Prophet Muhammad, perhaps the most important influence exerted by the tiny city was the Arabic language and the way the language came to be spoken all over Arabia — for it was the Arabic spoken in Makkah that became the classical standard for the language in other centres. As it is the language of the Qur'an, it continues to exert a stabilising influence on the spoken language.

At this time, leading Islamic personalities were dispatched to the Persian and Byzantine empires to spread the new faith. Within a century, through these envoys, the Makkan dialect had reached as far as the Pyrenees in the west and the frontiers of China in the east. Indeed, the Caliphate from Makkah, based in Damascus, came to rule an empire larger than that of ancient Rome. With the annual Pilgrimage, the city of Makkah was revived, the Caliphs appearing at the head of the pilgrims. Following the conquest of Iraq, western Arabia suffered an economic decline. Indian trade resumed its old route by the Persian Gulf and the valley of Euphrates.

The Umayyad Dynasty AH40-132 (660-749CE)

Conditions improved, however, under the Umayyad dynasty, led by Mu'awiya, a native of Makkah. The son of Abu Sufyan, who had fought the Prophet at the battle of Badr, he showed a keen interest in his home town, erected buildings, developed agriculture in its environs, dug new wells and constructed dams. His successors, the Marwanids, made Makkah a city of pleasure and ease. Exiles returning to take up residence

brought added wealth with them. Their exposure to external civilization had refined their tastes, making them accustomed to baths, a luxury requiring an abundant supply of water. This had to be carried from the nearby hills of Sarat — a new undertaking instituted by Khalid al-Kasri.

To mend the ravages of floods, the Caliphs Umar and Uthman erected barrages in the high-lying quarters, with the assistance of Christian engineers. They also buttressed the area around the Kaba'ah with barriers built at different levels to break the force of the flood. Their main aim was to protect the Kaba'ah. Unfortunately, their efforts failed: the slopes were too steep and the Batha basin had no outlet. And when they modified the plan, more buildings had to be pulled down.

Later attempts were made to enlarge the court around the Kaba'ah. The Umayyad Caliph prepared a plan for a great mosque — Masjid al-Haram — giving it galleries and a vast courtyard. Prominent among the Umayyads were Said bin al-As and two future Caliphs, Marwar bin al-Hakam and Umar bin Abd al-Aziz. In the absence of an Umayyad, the burden fell upon experienced officials like Hajjaj and Khalid al-Kasri, who were assigned to Taif and were transferred to Makkah. The centre of government, however, remained in Madinah which, under the Umayyad, surpassed Makkah in political importance, becoming the home of a new Muslim aristocracy.

Under Yazid I, the rise of Abd Allah bin al-Zubayr attracted Syrian troops to the Court of the Mosque, where the Kaba'ah was protected by scaffolding which caught fire through carelessness attributed to a soldier. Ibn Zubayr, an Islamically motivated anti-dynastic activist, restored the Kaba'ah to its pre-Islamic size, which remains unaltered. Later, however, he was outnumbered and massacred by the ruthless Al-Hajjaj bin Yusuf. In AH129 (747CE), a Khariji rebel from Yemen seized Makkah unopposed. He did not take permanent possession, for he was later defeated and slain by the troops of the Caliph Marwah II. In AH132 (750CE), Makkan, with the rest of the Caliphate, passed into the Abbasid Empire. When Marwah II was defeated, he was pursued to Egypt and killed.

Left: More than a million pilgrims crowd inside and outside the Great Mosque at the call to prayer, prostrating themselves in the great courtyard.

Below: One of the soaring graceful minarets of the Great Mosque rises above the Kaba'ah.

The Abbasids Period AH132-350 (750-961CE)

The Muslim Empire continued to grow and, under the Al-Masur AH136 (754CE), Spain was conquered and Baghdad founded, while Makkah itself continued much the same as it was under Umayyad rule. From the first century AH, Arabia had a number of allied groups who "fished in troubled waters" as brigands attacking caravans.

The decline of the Abbasid Caliphate and the death of Ma'mun saw a period of anarchy in Makkah, often followed by famine. Fighting broke out following representation by rulers at the Hajj to have their flags hoisted on Mount Arafat. Fifty years before the foundation of the Sharifate, the Qarmations created misery for Makkans, who had no adequate forces. From AH304 (916CE), the Qarmations barred the way to the pilgrims' caravans. In AH317 (930CE), 1,500 of them raided Makkah. They massacred the Makkans by the thousand, carrying with them the Black Stone to Bahrain. When in AH338 (950CE) they realised their inability to destroy Islam, they returned the Black Stone to Makkah. At that time, the Makkan Alids assumed the title of Sharif, which they have retained ever since.

The Musawis Dynasty

The ascendancy of the Sharifate saw Makkah take precedence over Madinah. The Sharifate asserted Makkah's independence by refusing homage to the Fatimid Caliph, who responded by besieging the town and cutting off vital imports of food supplies from Egypt. The Makkans had no choice but to surrender and Abu'l-Futuh set himself up as Caliph in AH384-432 (994-1039CE) to assert further the Sharifate's independence. It is believed he was influenced in this undertaking by al-Hakim's heretical innovations in Egypt. Al-Hakim, the Fatimid Khalifah in Egypt, quickly reduced the former's influence, forcing him to return to Makkah, only to find his powers there usurped by his relatives. He made a deal with al-Hakim to expel his relatives.

The Musawis dynasty ended with the death of Shukr AH432-453 (1039-1060CE), who had no male heirs, causing a struggle in the Hasanid

family, which badly affected Makkah. But when the Banu Shuaiba family went to the extreme of confiscating precious metals from the Kaba'ah for their private use, the Yemen ruler, al-Sulaihi, intervened, restoring order and security in the city. However, intervention by a foreigner annoyed the Hasanids, who persuaded al-Sulaihi to install one of their own members. Al-Sulaihi agreed to appoint Abu Hashim Muhammad AH455-598 (1063-1200CE) a Grand Sharif, founding the dynasty of the Hawashim.

The Hawashim Dynasty: AH455-598 (1063-1200CE)

Early in his reign, Abu Hashim, one of two brothers, fourth-generation descendants of Musa II, the ancestor of the Musawis, engaged in a protracted struggle with the Sulaimani branch, who felt humiliated by his appointment. Abu Hashim's decision to allow mention in the *khutba*, the Friday sermon, to the highest bidder, the Fatimid Caliph or the Saljuk Sultan, however, was opposed by Makkans. Once the official mention in the khutba was replaced by one of the Caliph, Egyptian imports were halted. This angered the Saljuk Sultan, who dispatched a group of Turkomans to Makkah.

This animosity between the Sultan and the Sharif inflicted great misery on pilgrims, particularly those from Iraq. Abu Hashim did not hesitate to plunder at his pleasure the pilgrim caravans from Iraq, which were led by Turkish officers. His successor continued this looting. By AH581 (1185CE), however, the Hawashim were losing control. Ten years earlier, the Ayubid dynasty had succeeded the Fatimids in Egypt, and was trying to extend its power as far as Asia.

On his way through Makkah, Saladin's brother gave up his plans to abolish the Sharifs, but gave the place of honour in Hajj to the Ayubids, whose names were then mentioned in the khutba after those of Abbasid Caliph and Sharif. The Ayubids issued coins in AH581 with Saladin's name and disciplined the Sharif's bodyguard, which was unruly. The Ayubid suzerainty enabled the Sharifate to become predominant. In all other respects, however, the state of affairs in Makkah improved only slightly.

The Katada to Wahhabi Period

Katada, Musa's descendant, succeeded in extending both his estates and influence from Yanub to Makkah, where he gained much support. It was his son, Hanzala, who prepared the groundwork for an attack on Makkah and seized the city while the inhabitants were performing an *Umrah* to commemorate the reconstruction of the Kaba'ah by Abd Allah bin al-Zubayr. Though he strove to make the territory an independent principality, Hanzala did not succeed. At the time, the Hijaz was open to overt political rivalries and Hanzala ruined his chances by brutally ill-treating the son of Ayubid al-Malik al-Adil AH540-615 (1145-1218CE). He angered the Caliph by his attacks on the Iraqi pilgrims, though later he managed to appease him. The envoy he sent to Baghdad returned with gifts and an invitation to visit Baghdad. On this occasion, he expressed, in verses, his policy of "splendid isolation", which was included in prose in his will.

Katada supported strongly an Imam of Hasanid descent in founding the Yemen Kingdom. After the reconquering of this region by a grandson of al-Adil, the Ayubids of Egypt, Syria and South Arabia were honoured by being mentioned in the khutba in Makkah along with the Caliph and Sharif. Katada was assassinated in a massacre carried out by his son Hasan, who wanted to eliminate family rivals. Hasan was frustrated in his ambition by the Ayubid prince Mas'ud, who appointed his own generals to govern Makkah. When Mas'ud died, power returned to the Sharifs, whose territory was allowed independence by the rulers of Yemen, to act as a buffer against Egypt.

By the middle of the seventh century AH, a number of changes had taken place in the world of Islam. In 1258CE, Hulagu ravaged Baghdad, bringing to an end the Abbasid Caliphate. Pilgrim caravans from Iraq no longer aroused political protests. The Mamluks in Egypt assumed power from the Ayubids. Sultan Baibars AH658-676 (1260-1277CE) soon became the most powerful ruler in the Islamic world. He let Makkah govern itself independently under the Sharif, Abu Numaiy, because he

Previous pages: The maghrib prayers at the Great Mosque in Makkah.

himself was a strong personality who ruled firmly in the second half of the 13th century CE. Numaiy's long reign firmly entrenched the power of the descendants of Katada.

Half-a-century after his death, the era was marked by various claims to his throne. The ensuing reign of Ajlan was full of political unrest, to the extent of provoking the Mamluk Sultan to threaten once to eliminate all the Sharifs. In 1361CE, Ajlan appointed his son and heir-apparent, Ahmad, co-regent, hoping to stave off a fratricidal struggle after his death. One of Ajlan's successors, a son, Hasan (1396-1426CE), tried to extend his power to the whole Hijaz area and to secure his financial interests.

Of the three sons of Hasan who had vied for his position during his lifetime, Barakat 1 was picked by the Sultan as co-regent. He succeeded his father 20 years later. He had to submit to the Sultan, who sent a permanent garrison of 50 Turkish horsemen under an Emir to Makkah. This Emir marked the beginning of the later governors who became highly influential under the Turkish suzerainty.

Barakat died in 1455CE after a fairly successful reign. Under the reign of his son, Muhammad (1455-1497CE), which coincided with Kait Bey's in Egypt, Makkah prospered. Bey left a fine memorial, in the form of several buildings he erected in Makkah.

Muhammad's son Barakat II (1497-1525CE) was an able and brave leader in quelling the struggle of the relatives around him, without Egyptian backing. But under his reign, the Ottoman Sultan conquered Egypt in 1517CE, changing the political map of the Islamic world. Constantinople (Byzantium) replaced Baghdad in importance, but there was no understanding between the Arabs and Turks. Still, Makkah under Sharifs Muhammad Abu Numaiy (1526-1566CE) and Hasan (1566-1601CE) remained in peace. The Ottoman protection extended the territory of the Sharifs as far as Khaybar in the north, Hali in the south and Najd in the east.

Makkah's continued dependence on Egypt fluctuated according to the strength of the government in Constantinople. The city depended on Egypt for supplies and on the Ottoman Empire for religious and educational matters, which attracted strong, interested patrons among

Left: The interior of the Prophet's Mosque.

Below: A cool shrine in the Prophet's Mosque, of grand beauty and intricate design.

Opposite: The green dome built in 1860 under the patronage of the Turkish Caliph Abd al Mejid.

the Sultans of Turkey. The Ottoman suzerainty intervened in the administration of justice. As the Sharifs had adopted the Shafi'i *madhhab*, or school of Islamic law, a Shafi'i *Kadhi* was the chief judge, coming for centuries from the same family. The highest bidder was sent annually from Constantinople.

Hasan died, leaving confusion and civil strife in Makkah. Descendants of Abu Numaiy were divided and claimed parcels of territory and often independence from the Grand Sharif. This struggle for supremacy with the officials of the Ottoman suzerain took place in the 17th century CE around the Abadila, the *Dhawi Zaid* and the *Dhawi Barakat*.

An energetic leader, Zaid (1631-1666CE) was intolerant of almost every act of the Turkish officials. However, he was unable to overcome differences between the Sunni Turks and the Shia Persians who had reached Makkah. The differences, which bordered on animosity, were created by an order of Sultan Murad to expel all Persians from the holy city, forbidding them to make future Pilgrimages. Both the Sharifs and the members of the upper-class Makkans were displeased by this stern measure. It only helped the mobs to plunder the rich Persians. Though the Turkish governor ordered them to go, the Sharifs allowed the Shias to make the Pilgrimage and to continue their stay in the city. The Sharifs also favoured the Zaids because they, too, had often been barred from Makkah by the Turks. The ensuing history of Makkah to the start of the Wahhabi period was made up of struggles among the Sharifan families themselves and between Ottoman officials in Makkah and in Jeddah.

The Wahhabi Period

In 1799CE, Ghalib (1788-1813CE) signed a treaty with the Emir of Dariya, defining the boundaries of their territories. The treaty stipulated that the Wahhabis would be allowed access to the holy city — but there were misunderstandings. Four years later, in 1803CE, the army of the Emir Saud approached Makkah. Ghalib withdrew to Jeddah and thereafter, in April, Saud entered Makkah, destroying *qubas*, and burning tobacco pipes and musical instruments.

Ghalib returned to Makkah in July, only to find himself gradually

walled in by enemies. A siege which began a month later was followed by famine and plague. By the following February, Ghalib was forced to accept Wahhabi suzerainty over his own position.

In 1807CE, when the Wahhabis sent back pilgrim caravans from Syria and Egypt, Muhammad Ali was instructed to deal with the Hijaz after finishing with Egypt. In 1813CE, he confronted Ghalib in Makkah. Though Ghalib made cautious advances, he was trapped by Muhammad Ali and his son Tusun, who took Makkah. Ghalib was exiled to Salonika, where he died in 1816CE. Muhammad Ali installed Ghalib's nephew Yahya bin Sarur (1813-1827CE) as Sharif, ending the Wahhabist rule over Makkah, while the Hijaz reverted once again to dependency on Egypt. Muhammad Ali revived the pious foundations, which lay in ruins, resumed the corn consignments and allotted stipends to those who had distinguished themselves in religion or other traditions. For these honourable acts, he is still remembered in Makkah.

Events in Makkah forced Muhammad Ali to intervene again in the domestic affairs of the Sharif. Following Yahya's vengeful act on one of his relatives, the viceroy deposed the Dhawi Zaid and installed Abadila Muhammad bin Awn (1827-1851CE) who, even though he succeeded in overcoming the customary struggle with relatives, faced problems with Muhammad Ali's deputy, resulting in their both being recalled to Cairo in 1836CE.

After a treaty between Turkey and Muhammad Ali in 1840CE, in which the Hijaz came under the former, the Sharif Muhammad bin Awn returned home, resuming the same position. As Ottoman suzerainty was vested in the person of the Wali of Jeddah, friction developed between the Wali and Muhammad bin Awn, whose friendship with Muhammad Ali proved useful to the Wali. The Wali pleased the Turks for his expeditions against the Wahhabi chiefs in Faisal al-Rayad and against the Asir tribe. The head of the Dhawi Zaid, Abd al-Muttalib (1851-1856CE), relying on his friendship with the grand vizier, engineered the overthrow of the Abadila in favour of his own group. When Abd al-Muttalib failed to develop good terms with one of the two pashas with whom he had to deal in Constantinople, the Wali cancelled his appointment, recalling Muhammad bin Awn in 1855CE. Muhammad

bin Awn re-entered the Sharifate in 1856CE, reigning for barely two years. He died in March 1858CE.

Abd Allah's rule (1858-1877CE) was a peaceful one and his subjects liked him. The opening of the Suez Canal in 1869CE freed the Hijaz from Egypt, but increased its connection with Constantinople. Its contacts with the wider world were improved by the installation of a telegraphic service. His elder brother, Husain, who was also popular, reigned only briefly (1877-1880CE) before he was assassinated by an Afghan.

Abd al-Muttalib, then ageing, was sent from Constantinople to succeed him (1880-1882CE). When his rule turned out to be oppressive, notables petitioned for his deposition. In 1881CE, Uthman Nuri Pasha, an energetic garrison commander, was sent with troops to Hijaz, charged with arranging the restoration of the Abadila. He outwitted Abd al-Muttalib, who was defeated in 1882CE and placed under house arrest in Makkah, where he remained until his death in 1886CE.

Uthman Pasha was rewarded in July 1882CE by being appointed a Wali. Awn al-Rafik (1882-1905CE) was appointed grand Sharif with him. Immediately, a personality conflict developed between these two strong individuals, who shared the same power in the administration of justice and the supervision of the safety of pilgrims. This friction led to the dismissal of Uthman in 1886CE. He was succeeded by Jamal Pasha, followed shortly by Safwaft Pasha. Only Ahmad Ratib, prone to material advantages, was shrewd enough to overlook some of the grand Sharif's acts and thereby secure his position by Awn al-Rafik's side. However, when al-Rafik died, it was an Abadila, Abdilahi, close friend of Uthman Pasha, who was picked as his successor. But fate intervened. He died even before starting his journey from Constantinople to Makkah. Awn al-Rafik was finally succeeded by his nephew Ali (1905-1908CE). In 1908CE, he and Ahmad Ratib were swept from their positions by the Turkish Revolution.

The last Sharif to come to power was Husain (1908-1916CE), also a nephew of Awn al-Rafik, whose reign was affected by the Great War, in

Previous pages: The Mosque of the Prophet Muhammad in the enchanting serenity of Madinah at dusk.

which Turkey was fully involved. Taking advantage of this situation, Husain declared himself independent in 1916CE, in an attempt to extend his power to its limits, first as the *Munkidh*, liberator of the Arabs then, on 22 June 1916CE, as king of the Hijaz or of Arabia, and finally Caliph. In September 1924CE, however, the Sultan of Najd, Abd al-'Aziz al-Saud, a descendant of the Wahhabi, led his troops to take Taif and — in October — Makkah.

King Husain fled to the Akaba and later to Cyprus, in May 1925CE, while his son Ali retired to Jeddah. Though Ibn Saud held Makkah and Madinah at siege for a year, he avoided bloodshed and complications with the European powers, until the two cities surrendered to him in December 1925CE.

From January 1926CE, Ibn Saud became King of the Hijaz, which, in 1932CE, was the renamed Kingdom of Saudi Arabia, now a powerful modern state with a jurisdiction that extends over 2,300,000 square kilometres.

In 1958CE, King Feisal bin Abd al 'Aziz al-Saud succeeded his brother, becoming a popular king in the Arab world and internationally, until his assassination by a nephew on 26 March 1975CE *(Rabi-ul-Awwal*, AH1395). Feisal was succeeded by his brother, King Khalid bin Abd al 'Aziz al-Saud, who died on 13 June 1982CE (20 *'Sha'ban*, AH1402) and was succeeded by his brother, King Fahd.

Below: The long day has ended and the lights on the Arafat Mosque twinkle above the tents.

3. The Kaba'ah

"Lo! The first sanctuary appointed for mankind was that at Makkah, a blessed place, a guidance to the peoples; wherein are plain memorials of God's guidance; the place where Ibrahim stood up to pray; and whosoever entereth it is safe . . ."

Qur'an III-96/97

*"Remember: We made the house a place of assembly
and a place of safety.
And take ye the station of Ibrahim
as a place of prayers.
We covenanted with Ibrahim and Ismael
that they should sanctify My House
for those who compass it round, or use it
as a retreat, or prostrate themselves
(thereon in prayer)."*

Qur'an II/125 and 127

Cradled in one of the desert alleys of Makkah, known as Wadi Ibrahim, lies the Kaba'ah, or the cube, from the Arabic origin, based on its shape. There the Kaba'ah has stood, indomitable for thousands of years, guarded by the encircling peaks of the Sarat mountains.

According to Islamic tradition, it was Adam who laid the foundation-stone of this House of God. It was to this very stone that the Prophet Ibrahim was guided with his family. And it was there that he left his wife Hagar and infant son Ismael. Hagar's desperate search for drinking water, by running to and fro between the hills of Safa and Marwah, and her entreaties to God were rewarded by the sprightly flow of water from the ground just near the spot where she had laid Ismael. It was this well that came to be known as Zamzam.

Ibrahim was entrusted with the task of rebuilding the Ancient House. When Ismael returned to Makkah to rejoin his family, he was a young man of 20, carrying respect from members of the Bani Jurham tribe, who had come to live within reach of the new well. Assisted by Ismael, Ibrahim undertook the sacred job. They rebuilt an irregular trapezoid shape, 36 metres long in the north-west, 23 metres in the south-west, 23

metres wide and nine metres high. It was a difficult task for father and son, but the two laboured patiently, placing one rock on top of the other without mortar until they had completed the cubic stone structure.

Later, in the past long centuries, idolatrous beliefs prevailed and the structure was utilised by pagans who covered the outer walls with the pelts of sacrificial animals. Towards the end of the last pagan period, the temple was surrounded by large houses of the stature of mansions, owned by wealthy Makkans. These houses had alleys that led directly to the Kaba'ah.

The interior walls of the edifice were covered with sacred stones, idols and other skeletal objects of pagan worship. On the ceiling and columns of the Kaba'ah hung pictures of prophets, angels, idols and trees, all of which were removed and destroyed at the start of the Islamic Era.

The ensuing years since those early days of Islam have seen the Kaba'ah treated with increasing reverence as more and more pilgrims travel, many of them for thousands of miles, to kneel in prayer before it. Even on ordinary, non-Hajj days, at the appointed hours of prayer five times each day, from the traditional first cock-crow of dawn to sunset, the Holy Kaba'ah attracts thousands of worshippers.

Throughout the world at such appointed times, millions of Muslim worshippers turn in unison to face the direction of the Kaba'ah in solemn prayer. The Kaba'ah, therefore, is the focus of prayer worldwide — Islam's most revered shrine. In Islam, across the world, it is known as the '*Qiblah*' direction, which unites all Muslims. The Kaba'ah exerts a unique spiritual hold.

Such a constant stream of worshippers means that the Kaba'ah is constantly surrounded. Tradition says that, even if it were possible for humans to stay away from the Kaba'ah, it could never be alone — for it is believed that, with or without worshippers, 70,000 guardian angels circle it in celestial attendance. Signs of their presence are betrayed by the ruffling of the rug that covers it. Religious love says that angels await the trumpet of the Last Day of Judgement, when they will glide to heaven with the Kaba'ah.

In the early years, following Prophet Muhammad's birth, Yemeni soldiers launched an attack — spearheaded with elephants — on Makkah

Above: Time exposure creates a blur of colour as pilgrims circle the Kaba'ah.

with the intention of destroying the Kaba'ah, but failed because of divine intervention. In the 17th century of the Christian Era, it was damaged by a storm which also affected other parts of Makkah. The Kaba'ah stands on a 61-centimetre base with a sharply inclined plane. It has a flat roof which, from a distance, gives it the appearance of a perfect cube. Its only door, opened two or three times a year, is located on the north side, about two metres above the ground.

In AH64, when the Kaba'ah was rebuilt by Ibn Zubayr, Chief of Makkah and nephew of Aysha, it had two doors, level with the ground mosque. According to Azraky, quoted by Burckhardt, a new door — taken there from Constantinople in 1633CE — was covered with silver and gilt ornaments, upon which were placed lighted candles, perfuming pans filled with musk, and aloe woods.

The position and function of the doors of the Kaba'ah have changed occasionally but for most of the time there has been only one door, located in the north-east façade. The present door is now about two metres above the ground, with mountings of silver and gold. This door is opened annually to wash the interior. To enter, a special stair is brought to the level of the door. The inside of the Kaba'ah is washed with water from the Zamzam well, and this holy chore is carried out — with a broom made of palm leaves — by the King of Saudi Arabia, aided by selected dignitaries. After that, the interior is sprinkled with perfume.

To the west of the Kaba'ah, 61 centimetres below the top, is a water spout, the *myzab*, which drains away the rainwater that collects on the roof of the Kaba'ah. At its mouth hangs "the beard of the myzab", a gilt board, on which the water falls. The spout is said to have come from Constantinople in AH826. It is made from various coloured stones and forms a handsome mosaic. There are also two large slabs of verd-antique in the centre. According to Makrizi, these were sent from Cairo in AH241. At this place, where it is customary for pilgrims to offer two *rak'ats* of *sala'at* (prayer), the wife and son of Ibrahim, Hagar and Ismael, lie buried. At the west side of this stands a semicircular wall whose two extremities are in line with the sides of the Kaba'ah. An opening, one-and-a-half metres wide, which is a short distance away, leads to the grave of Ismael. The area within these walls is called *Hajar Ismael*.

Pilgrims may enter the Kaba'ah. They may, however, affirm that they have prayed in it while prostrating themselves in the enclosure of the Hatym. The wall of the Hatym is built of solid stone nearly two metres high and over a metre thick, enclosed in white marble inscribed with prayers in Arabic letters neatly engraved on the stone in modern characters. According to Burckhardt, these and the casing are the work of El-Ghoury, an Egyptian Sultan of AH917.

Since Ibrahim's days, almost 4,000 years ago, the Kaba'ah has remained standing in the same location, unchanged in form and on the same foundation. It is now an accepted historical fact that all reconstructions of the Kaba'ah were carried out on the same foundation. It has also been noted that the Kaba'ah was built of alternating courses of stone and teak. Thus, there was a total of 31 courses, 16 of stone, and 15 of wood, beginning and ending with a course of stone.

Left: Pilgrims push forward to touch the door of the Kaba'ah.

Below: A door-keeper crouches to guard the door of the Kaba'ah.

Below: The Tawaf, seven circuits around the Kaba'ah, is performed by all pilgrims, each circuit beginning opposite the Black Stone.

4. The Great Mosque of Makkah

The Kaba'ah is surrounded by an open courtyard which is central to the structures of the Great Mosque of Makkah, al-Masjid al-Haram. Originally, seven paved causeways from the colonnades led to the Kaba'ah in the centre of the courtyard. Raised above the ground, they were wide enough to allow four or five people to walk abreast. The area of the Mosque is on a lower level than its surrounding area. This staircase leads down from the gate on the north side on to the platform of the colonnade, which is about four paces from the south gate.

The Great Mosque is unique because it has no Qiblah, or *Mihrab*, as found in other Mosques. Worshippers praying in any of its wings simply face the Kaba'ah. Damage, demolition, renovation and expansion over the years have removed any trace of the Mosque's antiquity. The great interior walls enclosing the colonnades bear a simple Arabic inscription — the name of Muhammad and those of his companions, Abu Bakr, Omar, Othman and Ali. "Allah", in Arabic characters, is repeated in several places, while, inscribed on the exterior of the gates, the names commemorating the builders are amplified by lengthy details given by Makkan historians. On the south side, a clear inscription denotes *Bab al-Ibrahim*. The south side was rebuilt by the Egyptian Sultan El-Ghoury in AH906. *Bab Ali* and *Bab Abbas* bear a long inscription placed there by Sultan Murad ibn Suleiman in AH984, after he had repaired the whole building.

The terrain around the Masjid al-Haram has affected its history. The physical formation of the rocky hills has acted as a constraint on the form, growth and direction the Mosque would take. For a long time, the storm waters of the hills which drain the Makkan valley took their toll of the area. Only in modern times have better methods been utilised to stop the flooding.

Under Umar ibn Khattab AH17

When Umar visited Makkah to perform the Lesser Pilgrimage of Umrah, he found the Kaba'ah badly damaged by floods which also affected the Maqaam Ibrahim, and immediately ordered their repair. He enlarged the courtyard of the Kaba'ah, giving it a polygonal shape and enclosing

the Zamzam well, which entailed demolishing some of the houses around it, for which the owners were duly compensated. Umar also built a wall enclosing the Kaba'ah which, according to traditional sources, was not there during the time of the Prophet and Sayyid Abu Bakr. The wall built by Umar, which was less than the height of an average man, had a gate on which lamps were placed to illuminate the enclosure after dark. Umar built a dyke in an effort to try to prevent future flooding.

Under Uthman ibn Affan, AH26

As the third Caliph, Uthman extended the area accommodating the pilgrims even more, for their numbers had increased over the decade or so since Umar extended it. He, too, was forced to demolish more houses and compensated the owners accordingly. Uthman also renovated the Mosque and, for the first time, introduced covered porticos for prayers.

Under Abdullah ibn Zubayr, AH65

Zubayr, grandson of Abu Bakr, the first Caliph of Makkah, was locked in a political struggle with Yazid for the control of Makkah. When Yazid attacked the city, during a siege, the Kaba'ah caught fire and its walls crumbled. After Yazid's death, however, Zubayr reconstructed the Kaba'ah. His first task was to clear the Kaba'ah of the stones thrown by Yazid's forces, which were piled all over it. As the Kaba'ah was virtually destroyed, he ordered the remains to be demolished. Afraid of being cursed, Makkans refused at first to help, until ibn Zubayr himself initiated the demolition. The Black Stone had broken into three pieces and ibn Zubayr bound the pieces together with silver and kept it in his home until the walls were raised to the level of the original position of the stone. At this time, Ibrahim's original foundations "consisting of Cyclopean green stones" were found to be six cubits and a span longer than the demolished structure.

Ibn Zubayr thus increased and rebuilt the Kaba'ah's length from 18 to 26 cubits, and the height from 18 to 27 cubits, measured from the plinth, which was itself 50 centimetres high. The new structure, made of stone

Above: The interior of the Prophet's Mosque.

*Right: The ancient city of Makkah now has
many high-rise office blocks and hotels, but
the Sacred Mosque dominates the skyline.*

two cubits thick, had 27 courses. The Caliph built two doors 11 cubits high — one was in the east for entering, the other in the west was an exit. Some sources maintain that these doors were gold-plated. A wooden ladder at the north corner led to the roof. Traditional Yemenite building techniques of cut stone and mortar were used.

Mosaics from a Yemenite church built by Araha, an Abyssinian, and three polychromatic marble columns were also used. The interior was cleverly brightened by employing transparent marble, imported from San'a and built into the roof. And even though the Black Stone was not in place during the reconstruction, circumambulation went on around a temporary wooden structure. As soon as the walls had risen to the previous level of the Black Stone, however, it was set in place, with two stones firmly fixed to it. Both the inside and the outside of the walls of the Kaba'ah were draped with Coptic silk fabric, a tradition dating from Mu'awiya. Using a few remaining stones, a circular pathway, 10 cubits wide, was constructed around the Kaba'ah. These stones were washed with Zamzam water. The enclosure surrounding the sanctuary was enlarged. The existing walls were repaired and colonnades, roofed with plane wood, were introduced.

Under al-Hajjaj, AH74

The siege of the city by al-Hajjaj also damaged the Kaba'ah and, after gaining control of the city, al-Hajjaj pulled down the entire structure constructed by ibn Zubayr, rebuilding it seven cubits shorter, with only one door. He raised the other door four-and-a-half metres off the ground to restrict and control entry into the Kaba'ah and divided the façade of the building into three horizontal sections. The lowest, 20 metres high, contained the door to the interior. He added three fake doors under a cornice, one on each façade of the sanctuary. A false ceiling, built of logs, was also added. The logs protruded beyond the wall surface, on which was hung a curtain. Three red marble columns inside the building held up the long roof.

Under al-Walid, AH91

Al-Walid restored the Kaba'ah after flood damage. He enlarged the area of the Mosque and renovated the building, roofing the colonnades with ornamented teak beams and introducing glass mosaics, marble panelling, gilt spouts and crenellations. He was the first to utilise marble columns imported from Egypt and Syria.

Under the Umayyad Architectural Influence, up to AH132

The Umayyad Dynasty introduced a magnificent structure of cut stone and arcades resting on marble columns. The Umayyad building was splendidly decorated internally with marble panelling and mosaics, some of which were used in the reconstruction of the Masjid al-Haram.

Under the Abbasid Architectural Influence, AH132-656

The Abbasid period was marked by a decline in Syrian influence and an increase in San'aian Persian influence in architecture, characterised by axial planning and immensity of scale, with an emphasis on brick hidden by stucco. The four-centred arch appeared, to create a new form. Lustrous tiles were also introduced at this time.

Under Abu Jafar al-Mansur, AH137

Al-Mansur made a significant contribution by extending the northern and western sides of the Mosque, doubling the size of previous extensions.

Under Muhammad al-Mehdi: AH161-164

Al-Mehdi made two successive extensions. One, in AH161, on the northern side, displaced buildings to create additional space. This extra space on one side only meant the Kaba'ah no longer stood at the centre and, when al-Mehdi realised this during the AH164 Hajj, he ordered

further extensions on the southern side. In order to ensure that the Kaba'ah remained directly in the centre of the courtyard, he supervised the work from a vantage point on Mount Abu Qubais.

Al-Mehdi built three rows of covered marble and stone colonnades surrounding the courtyard. The columns were covered by a teak roof. He also added four small wooden buildings for prayers, one for each of the four *Imams* of the four Orthodox Jurisprudic schools. Unfortunately, al-Mehdi did not live to see the end of the project he had started. He was succeeded by his son, Musa al-Hadi, who finished the extensions in AH167. During his reign, Musa al-Hadi gave the mosque its maximum size. Except for the addition of *Bab al-Ziyada* and Bab al-Ibrahim, nothing was added to the area until the recent extension, al-Mehdi's construction thus remaining unchanged for six centuries.

However, innovations between the years AH222 and AH486 saw yellow stone columns from Samaria erected for the arcades, while green and polychrome marble were set in the north-west corner of the Kaba'ah. To protect it from the weather, the Maqaam Ibrahim was gilded and placed under a wooden structure. Wooden lampposts went up around the Kaba'ah. Continuing flood damage, however, necessitated further repairs and green marble was used to cover the top of the Kaba'ah. The silver gate was plated with gold. Inside, a band of gold embossing, about one metre wide, was added. A red silk curtain bearing gold inscriptions covered the Kaba'ah.

In AH284, Moqtadir al-Abbasi incorporated a part of the *Dar al-Nadwah* into the Mosque. When its remaining part was included later, it was named Bab al-Ziyada. In AH306, al-Abbasi added the Bab al-Ibrahim to the area, which it had occupied up to the year AH1375. By AH442, according to one pilgrim, the three Umayyad columns were still in place, while the alabaster panes of the entablature had been replaced by glass. At each corner was a high recess in which lay a Qur'an. The walls were inlaid with gold slabs. On the northern wall were six silver Mihrabs.

Previous pages: The great courtyard of the Sacred Mosque is filled with more than 500,000 people at a time during the Pilgrimage.

Pieces of wood believed to have come from Noah's Ark were set in silver and hung on the walls. From then, for 500 years until the start of the Ottoman Empire, the Kaba'ah and the Masjid al-Haram hardly changed.

Under Farj ibn Barqouq, AH802-807

A fierce fire which broke out in AH802, during the reign of Farj ibn Barqouq, a Sharaksa king, destroyed the whole of the western side of the Mosque, including more than 100 marble pillars, and completely ruined the roof. Amir Besaq al-Zahiri undertook the repair of the damage.

The Ottoman Mosque, From AH979 Onwards

In AH979, Ottoman King Sultan Salim commissioned the great Turkish architect, Sinan, to carry out large-scale renovation of the entire Masjid al-Haram. The dismantling of the Masjid began in AH980, from the *Bab al-Salaam*. Construction of the new building started when the first 982 columns of the colonnade surrounding the Kaba'ah were replaced by marble and stone columns. These were arranged in such a way as to support the stuccoed stone arches and cupolas. Some 500 Ottoman-style domes replaced the flat roof. Later, Abdullah Mufti decorated the interior of the domes with gold motifs and calligraphic compositions.

In AH994, in accordance with Sinan's plan, Sultan Salim extended the courtyard to 164 metres by 168 metres. The paving around the Kaba'ah was replaced by polychrome marble, extra palm-shaped lamps were placed in the courtyard and a seventh minaret was added.

Early 19th century visitors noted that the floor was paved with large stones and seven paved causeways led from the Mosque to the Kaba'ah. The floor of the Mosque was well below street level and entry was through stairways from 19 entrances. By then, there were seven minarets. The inside of the Mosque was filled with about 500 columns, with the eastern side containing four rows of columns. The other three sides had three rows each. The columns were joined by pointed arches.

In the year AH1039, flooding caused two cornerstones of the Kaba'ah

Ablaze with neon lights and lines of slow-moving traffic, night-time Makkah profiles the beauty of traditional Islamic architecture against modern Makkah.

to collapse and it was agreed to repair it. Excavations were carried out and stopped only when the stones of the foundations of Ibrahim were reached.

The New Kaba'ah

The new Kaba'ah, constructed on the very foundations of Ibrahim, made extensive use of the previous masonry. The inside columns of the Kaba'ah were coated with gold, and a silver door was presented by Sultan Suleiman. The Kaba'ah was then covered with two pieces of cloth, the first red and on top of it a black one. The sand around the Kaba'ah was washed in Zamzam water. The Kaba'ah and the Masjid al-Haram remained this way for 400 years, until King Abd al'-Aziz's AH1375 project to extend and rebuild the Masjid al-Haram began.

While in the past the Masjid al-Haram was integrated with the city, it is now segregated by roads, plazas and parking areas and incorporates a flood-diversion system.

The area around the side of the Mosque was gradually cleared in the AH1380s (1960sCE) and today it is detached from the hills and surrounding buildings.

The contrast between the size of the Masjid al-Haram and the congestion in the town is enormous. Those who approach the Masjid al-Haram find the scale of this beautiful grey-and-white marble building overwhelming. For those who visit it for the first time, the anticipation of seeing the Kaba'ah heightens their delight at the sight of the exterior. Major and minor gateways create a feeling of openness, ever welcoming the visitor. Because of its vast scale, however, most can only grasp a few aspects of its features at a time.

It took 20 years in four phases to build the new Masjid al-Haram. In the first phase, the section between the hills of *al-Safa* and *al-Marwah* was built over the existing pathways, covered by galvanised metal roofs. Initially, only a concrete frame was erected, with a sample of the stonework placed in 11 bays.

Phase two saw the outer octagon of the new Mosque completed. Excavations revealed that the natural ground level, some four metres

below the existing ground level, was filled with the debris of demolished houses, and the space was used for a basement, which had not been included in the original plan. In this phase, the area for the circumambulation of the Kaba'ah, or *mataf,* was extended and the stairways to the Zamzam well were built.

When phase three was under way, King Feisal bin Abdul Aziz al-Saud modified Gaveni's original plans and retained the Ottoman mosque, a decision which was made after a major conference of Muslim architects and engineers who met in Makkah in AH1387 (1962CE) to consider possible alternatives. King Feisal wisely felt that the integration of the new with the old Ottoman structure would give a sense of continuity and Gaveni developed an "infill"— of peripheral roads, shops and squares.

The renovation of the Haram was completed with phase four. Its corners were bevelled to accept three diagonal entrance gates. The new Masjid al-Haram marked one of the world's most significant architectural accomplishments. As one of the largest and most impressive religious buildings in the world, it ranks with the Church of St Peter in Rome, St Paul's Cathedral in London and the Aghra Sophia in Istanbul.

The circulation spaces, which are five metres wide and defined by a dark marble floor pattern, contrast subtly with the white marble of the places of prayer, which each cover 15 square metres. In elevation, the circulation way is composed of arches set on square columns of black marble, while the prayer places are built in flat, covered structures set on white circular columns. However, the orderly use of space is not followed all the time, especially during the Hajj, when any and every space is set aside for prayer.

The basement occupies 31,200 square metres, a large part of which is for prayers, while there are 250 utility rooms, endowment areas of the *Zamzamis,* those who provide water for the pilgrims, and walkways and steps for ascending to the Mosque.

The ground floor has two parts, a covered area inside and a raised part, for plazas, located on the exterior periphery. The inside area, which covers 46,100 square metres, is made up of gateways, circulation and prayer places, five corner offices, opening to the exterior staircases, and the first level of al-Safa and al-Marwah. The floor plane lowers to

Left: His late Majesty King Khalid Ibn Abdul Aziz kneels in prayer at the station of Abraham, on the very spot Abraham chose to pray to God.

Below: The lighting by night lends a special beauty to the Mosque at Makkah.

the courtyard in three levels, each about a metre lower than the other, providing a more-or-less uninterrupted view of the Kaba'ah, the focus of the Haram. The open areas around the Haram measure about 13,250 square metres and are surrounded by shops and toilet facilities.

The first floor, some 12 metres above the ground floor, is linked by 13 staircases. Four bridges connect the north and east gates to the upper outer road levels and provide access to the first-floor level. The area, which measures 46,100 square metres, is identical with the ground floor, but there are no offices. The top of each of the three main gates is allocated to a *madrasah* (school). The entire floor is flat, except for the top of the Safa-Marwah section where there is a series of stairways. The first-floor level of the Safa-Marwah now serves the same purpose for the ritual of *Sa'y* as the ground floor, thus doubling the capacity for this important aspect of the Hajj.

The mosque's flat roof — on which there are three main gateways and seven minarets, the Safa-dome, and the pitched roof of the rectangular Marwah space — is used for water storage and filtration tanks and no pilgrims are allowed in this area.

The planners' concept is that of the sacred treasure, the Kaba'ah, hidden within the surrounding hills. Thus the inner courtyard opens to the cosmos, where the Kaba'ah stands at the centre of the universe.

The overall view of this unique Mosque, therefore, begins on the hilltops and moves down through the seven great minarets to its two-storey, 24-metre-high walls, the dome of the old mosque, to follow gradually the descending line of the courtyard floor to the Kaba'ah.

The Masjid al-Haram has 96,650 individual prayer-mat places, while the old and renovated areas have 11,450 and the courtyard 23,350. During the Hajj, all available space, inside and out, is considered in determining its capacity. In this instance, the capacity reaches 400,000 prayer-mat places.

The decorative patterns of the Mosque are based upon a rich heritage of Islamic art, composed of geometry, arabesque and calligraphy. The geometric patterns start with the circle, symbol of perfection, inscribing the polygons. Other geometric patterns include the square, the octagon, the hexagon and the triangle. From these evolved the star, the rotating

square and the nine-square form. Though also geometric, the arabesque patterns evolve more freely in fluid shapes, simulating floral patterns. The lotus spiral, floral motif and other shapes are discreetly employed. Two main capitals are seen in the main prayer halls and circulation spaces. Other capitals are located on the exterior. As the circulation spaces are arched, they necessitate the first capital shape, a floral motif on which rests a square block. The other capital form is related to the main prayer spaces, except the flat roof structure. A highly ornate *midrib* motif sits on a geometric column head. Surface patterns, capitals, columns and stone veneers combine to create the harmonious panels which define the exterior. The brass and metal surface decoration of the doorways is in geometric patterns. The rectangular or square ceiling exhibits a central medallion of star octagons and a spiral of lotus motifs. Pale pink and ochre tones appear in the ceiling — the only use of colour apart from the gold leaf of the calligraphy, the white to black range of stones and occasional green roof tiles. Kufic script in bold gold leaf on an off-white background appears on the calligraphic motifs which are repeated throughout. Marble and marble tiles cover the entire 115,450 square metres of open areas, 60,000 square metres of walls, columns and parapets on the ground floor and first floor. And 68 stairways are covered with marble.

The Kiswah

The four walls of the Kaba'ah are always covered with a fine piece of cloth which has improved in quality over the years. The covering follows an ancient custom. In the pre-Islamic period, the Kaba'ah had two different coverings, one for winter and one for summer. The covering is known as the *kiswah*.

In the past, the cloth was furnished by the Sultan of Baghdad or came from Egypt or Yemen, depending on whose influence was greater in Makkah. Provision of the kiswah was considered proof of sovereignty over the Hijaz. When it was sewn in Constantinople, it used to cost in the region of £3,600, a substantial sum in those days. The material was a mixture of silk and cotton, dull black in colour, embroidered at about every

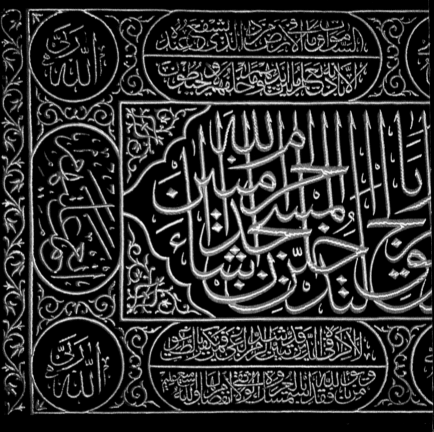

A separate, more heavily embroidered covering is made for the door of the Kaba'ah.

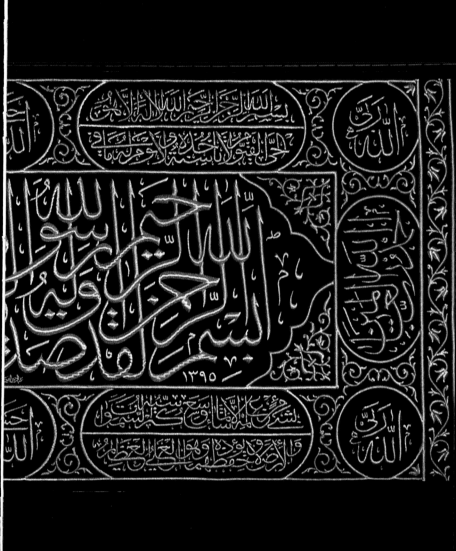

Above: The station of Abraham at the north-east side of the Kaba'ah.

Above: The Black Stone, Hajar al-Aswad, is set in a silver frame in the south-east corner of the Kaba'ah.

time, it was broken into three pieces and a number of fragments, now held together by a silver band.

Over the years, the surface has been worn down by the touch and kisses of millions of pilgrims. The stone itself is reddish-brown to black with yellowish particles. The border which surrounds it rises a little above the surface of the stone. Ali Bey described it mineralogically, as "a block of volcanic basalt, whose circumference is sprinkled with little crystals, pointed and straw-like, with rhombs of the tile-red upon a dark background, like velvet or charcoal, except one of its protuberances, which is reddish." Others have described it as meteorite stone, although one Muslim geologist was unable to place it among terrestrial rocks or meteorites. The walk around the Kaba'ah is performed as near the Black Stone as possible. Those who can do so reach, touch and kiss it, while those prevented from doing so by the flow of the pilgrims wave at it in salutation.

The Zamzam Well

When the Prophet Ibrahim had laid his son on the ground to rest and left him with his wife Hagar, with only a handful of dates and a leather gourd with some water, he wandered away into the Arabian desert. Hagar followed him and asked him if God had commanded him to leave them there. Ibrahim said he had, to which Hagar replied: "Then He will not let us go to waste."

Mother and son had neither sufficient food nor sufficient water to sustain them for even a few days, and on the third day in the heat of the valley began to feel extremely thirsty. When the infant Ismael cried for water, Hagar ran desperately to and fro between the foothills of al-Safa and al-Marwah, with her hands lifted to the heavens, all the time crying out appealingly: "O Thou Bountiful. Thou full of Grace! Who shall have mercy on us unless Thou hast mercy?"

In answer, the angel Jibreel appeared, striking the ground with his wing, at which spot water immediately gushed out, forming a stream which began to flow over the sand. According to one source, it was Hagar's joyful exclamation to her son, Ismael, in Egyptian —"*Zem, zem*"

"Stay, stay" — which earned the well its name. Hagar formed a wall of sand around the spring to stop it from flowing away. Another source has traced the name to "*Zam! Zam!*" — "Fill! Fill!" — Hagar's impatient cry when she saw the water.

In earlier times, the well was covered with a small square building crowned with a cupola, topped with a crescent and surfaced with marble. The water was drawn by four windlasses at the top of the shrine. However, at one point in its history, the Zamzam well was lost, until the grandfather of Prophet Muhammad, 'Abd al-Muttalib, relocated it through a dream. For years, writers have found it difficult to describe the exact taste of the Zamzam water. It has been described by one as slightly bitter. The writer quotes his guide in Makkah describing it thus: "Allah — may I be his sacrifice — has made this (Zamzam) water sacred, as you know. It is neither sweet nor bitter, neither scented nor stinking, but would appear in its taste to be a mixture of all these qualities. In everything sacred there must be a mystery . . . ."

Arabian and Persian literature is full of references to Zamzam water. Apart from being considered the purest water in the world, it is rated second only to Kauser, a heavenly stream in the Garden of Paradise that keeps the grass evergreen and the flowers ever-blooming. Some believe that the Zamzam water has curative properties when drunk by those of pure conscience. It is also considered to be inspiring, prolonging life and purifying the souls of the unswerving faithful. The present facilities of the Zamzam well are under the mataf line, on its outer extremity, with stairs leading down to it. Traditionally, the pilgrims draw some water from the Zamzam well and sprinkle themselves with it on the head, back and stomach, after which they drink a little, with the following prayer:

> *"O Lord, I beseech Thee to make this draught for me a source of inexhaustible knowledge, a vast livelihood, and a preventive of all pains and diseases."*

Above and Right:
Pilgrims cluster round a
stall for water from the
well of Zamzam, which
saved the lives of Hagar
and her son Ismael.

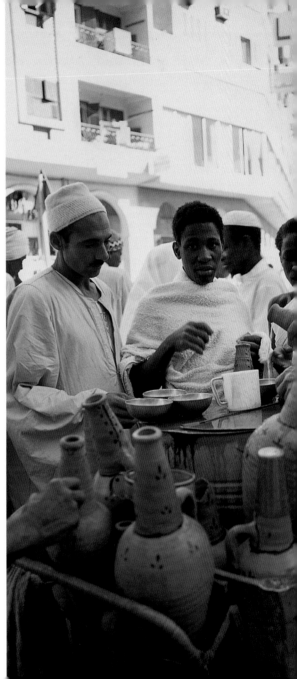

Below: Pilgrims pass through the great archways out of the Sacred Mosque into the crowded streets.

Al-Safa and al-Marwah

In remembrance of Hagar's desperation under the drive of thirst, millions of Muslims relive those difficult moments by running seven times between the two hills during Hajj, reciting aloud the same words uttered by Hagar in thankful relief:

> *"O Thou Bountiful, Thou full of Grace! Who shall have mercy on us unless Thou hast mercy?"*

This area, known as the *masa*, a subway-like lane between two hills, is now a covered two-floor space 400 metres long. The Safa side ends in a domed space, while the Marwah side has a rectangular, elevated roof space.

> *"And proclaim unto mankind the Pilgrimage. They will come unto thee on foot and on every lean camel: they will come from every deep ravine."*

Qur'an XXXII - 27

5. The Hajj: The Pilgrimage

Each year, millions of Muslims from all over of the world travel to the Holy City to perform the Pilgrimage or the Hajj, to fulfil the fifth pillar of Islam. (The other four are faith, *Shahada*; prayer, *Sala'at*; alms, *Zakat*; and fasting, *Ramadhan*.) All Muslim men and women who can afford to undertake the sacred journey at least once in a lifetime without creating any discomfort to their dependants are enjoined to fulfil the pillar, hence the reference to it sometimes as "The Journey of a Lifetime."

Those who intend to proceed on the Hajj are required to repent their past sins, clear their debts, and provide their dependants with sufficient funds to last them the duration of the Hajj, which might be anything from a month to two months. Whatever money the prospective pilgrim intends to use for this purpose must have been earned honestly.

On arrival in Makkah for either the Lesser Pilgrimage, Umrah, or the Hajj, the pilgrim traditionally bathes and wears perfume, trims his moustache, shaves pubic and armpit hair and pares his nails. He then dons the ihram, the Pilgrimage dress, which is a white piece of cloth, and a pair of unsewn slippers. Female pilgrims may wear any clothes as long as they do not imitate the male attire. They are required to avoid wearing clothes that might arouse the men emotionally or cause them to be distracted. After wearing the ihram, the pilgrims must declare their intention, that is whether they will be performing the Umrah or the Hajj. If the choice is for Umrah, the pilgrim recites:

"O God in Your service ready here I am for the Umrah."

If the pilgrim intends to perform the Hajj, he says:

"O God in Your service ready here I am for the Hajj."

If the choice is for both Umrah and Hajj, the pilgrim states:

"O God in Your service ready here I am for both Umrah and Hajj".

There are five appointed places, migrates, from which the Hajj or Umrah starts:

The Pilgrimage

Jabal al-Nur

HARAM

MAKKAH
The Sacred Mosque.
The Ka'bah.
Place of Abraham.
Well of Zamzam.

To Jeddah
45 miles.

Three
stone
pillars

MINA
Site of Abraham's
Temptation
and Sacrifice.

MUZDALIFAH

HARAM

**Jabal al-Rahmah
(Mount of Mercy)**
Site of Muhammad's
Farewell Sermon.

PLAIN OF ARAFAT

To Ta
30 mile

Above: Pilgrims from Malaysia assemble on deck as their chartered ocean liner arrives in Jeddah.

Below: Pilgrims walk across the tarmac in a seemingly never-ending stream from jetliners.

1. Dhul Halifa, Abyar Ali, for pilgrims from Madinah north;
2. Aljifa, for pilgrims from Palestine, Lebanon, Jordan and Syria;
3. Karn El-Manzil, for pilgrims from Najd;
4. Ylamlam, for pilgrims from Yemen;
5. Thatu Ariq, for pilgrims from Iraq.

These appointed places apply to those specific nationalities and to others who happen to pass through those regions. The pilgrim and the *Mu'tamer* (one intending to perform the Umrah) are required to perform the rituals of the ihram as they cross these points.

According to the Holy Qur'an, the Hajj has to be performed between the eighth and the 13th days of the 12th month of Dhu al-Hijjah, of the Muslim lunar calendar.

The choice of Pilgrimage governs the kind of ihram the pilgrim will wear. The first is for the great Hajj alone. For this the pilgrims wear the ihram until they complete all the rituals of the Hajj. While performing the Hajj, the pilgrim recites:

> *"O God, here I am for Thy service for Hajj, O God I am ready."*

The second is ihram for Umrah alone. The pilgrim must assume the ihram in the *miqat* and recite the *talbiyah*, or calling:

> *"O God, here I am for Thy service for Umrah (alone), O God, I am ready"*.

The pilgrim circles the Kaba'ah and runs between al-Safa and al-Marwah. Male pilgrims then shave their heads or shorten their hair, free themselves from the rites of the Umrah and remain so until the time of the Hajj.

The third kind of ihram is for the combined Pilgrimage for both the Umrah and the Hajj, for which the pilgrim is required to don the ihram at one of the marked places of entry while reciting:

> *"O God, ready in Your service here I am for both Hajj and Umrah."*

The pilgrim continues to wear the ihram until both the Hajj and the Umrah are completed. Alternatively, the pilgrims may assume the ihram and Hajj before the *tawaf*, or circumambulation, provided they have offered a voluntary gift in the form of an animal.

This is because the Muslim performing both the Hajj and Umrah is required to offer a sacrifice of some sort. If pilgrims are unable to make any gifts, they are required to fast for three days during the Pilgrimage and another seven days at home after the Pilgrimage. The three days of the fast are the seventh, eighth, and ninth of the month. If one wishes, one may also fast after taking off the ihram worn for Umrah. There is an alternative set of three days in case one cannot fast on the appointed days.

A female pilgrim who has her monthly period or is pregnant and is intending to perform the Umrah before circumambulation but does not wish to miss the Hajj can wear the ihram. She declares her intention to perform the Hajj, and jointly performs the Hajj and Umrah.

Immediately after assuming the ihram, the pilgrim recites the talbiyah or incantation for the pilgrims loudly:

> *"O God, here I am for Your service, ready I am. There is none equal to You, Here I am for Your service, ready I am. Indeed, all the blessings are for You and the Kingdom is Yours. There is none equal to You."*

Because the pilgrims seek to do no more than please Allah during the Pilgrimage, even companions to the Holy City have to be godly and charitable. Throughout the journey, the pilgrim must praise God, ask God's forgiveness, recite the Qur'an and perform sala'at or daily prayers jointly with the other pilgrims. Thus, reciting the talbiyah every now and then during the Pilgrimage is considered a duty. The incantation is supposed to be chanted in a very loud voice by the male pilgrim but only louly enough to be heard by her neighbour by the female pilgrim. The pilgrim's main objective is to seek God and thence to surrender, which is the literal translation of the word Qur'an.

The pilgrim is prohibited from doing certain things for the duration

Above: Pilgrims pour into Mina for Muzdalifah.

Opposite: Strangers who set out perhaps a month before the Pilgrimage from their respective countries have now become brothers in Islam.

of wearing the ihram. If the pilgrim breaks any of these prohibitions, they are required to offer certain sacrifices. The pilgrim is not allowed to shave, pare nails or wear perfumes, wear a shirt with saffron on it, be lewd, abusive or angry in conversation, indulge in sexual intercourse, flirt or hunt.

Pilgrims may carry luggage, wash their heads, clean and change their clothes and use a blanket as protection from the cold. The whole of the body may be covered with clothes, except the head and the ears. Men may wear rings, watches and glasses, but cannot wear sewn clothes or socks. A women must be accompanied by her husband or a close relative. If the pilgrim intentionally breaks any of these rules, they are required to offer compensation, known as *fidyah*. This ranges from fasting for a stipulated number of days, sacrificing a sheep and offering the meat to the poor, or feeding a given number of poor people. If any of these rules is broken inadvertently, however, no compensation is needed.

Entering Makkah

It is customary for pilgrims to bathe and spend the night in Thu Tuwa, near the Zahir, before entering the Holy City. Upon entering, pilgrims approach the Holy Mosque — the Masjid al-Haram, from Bab al-Salaam, the Gate of Peace, though they can also enter it through any of the other gates. On entering, the pilgrim recites:

> *"In the name of God, by God, from God, and for God, may Thou open the doors of Your Mercy for me."*

On approaching the Kaba'ah, the pilgrim recites:

> *"O My God, may Thou make Your Ancient House more glorified, more honoured, more feared and more loved. Praise be to God, Lord of the Worlds! Thank God, glorified be His name, Who enabled me to visit His Holy House and considered me worthy of it. Thank God in all circumstances. O My God, I have come to visit*

Your Holy House only because the Pilgrimage to it was made a duty by You. O God, may You be pleased with my Pilgrimage, forgive me, make all my action correct. There is no deity except God!"

The Tawaf: Circumambulation

The pilgrim performs the tawaf by circling the Kaba'ah anti-clockwise seven times, starting and finishing at the Black Stone. Before beginning the tawaf, the pilgrim holds part of the ihram under the right arm and the other part over the left shoulder. The first three circuits around the Kaba'ah are made at a jogging pace, the last four at a walking pace. Each time pilgrims pass the Black Stone, they are required to touch or kiss it, while reciting the Qur'anic verse:

"O Lord, award us good in this world, and in the hereafter protect us from the torture of hell."

Whenever a pilgrim approaches the Black Stone, they say "Allah-u-Akbar!", "God is the Greatest!" If it is possible, it is also desirable to kiss the Black Stone silently, as did the Prophet Muhammad. However, if it is not possible, they can raise both hands in salutation directed towards it. Facing the Black Stone, the pilgrim recites:

"In the name of God. God is the Greatest! O God, give me faith and acceptance of Your Book, and the fulfilment of my promise and following of the traditions of Your Prophet Muhammad, May Your Peace Be Upon Him."

Also, during the tawaf, it is desirable for the pilgrim to recite:

"O God, may You be pleased with my pilgrimage, reward my coming to You, forgive my sins and have mercy on me. O God, forgive my sins which You (and) only You know, You, the Kindest, the most Majestic!"

Above: A young girl reads the Qur'an, the holiest Islamic scripture, which is believed by all Muslims to contain the word of God as given to the Prophet Muhammad.

Opposite: Of the world's 800 million Muslims, more than a quarter live in Africa.

Failure to complete the seven circuits around the Kaba'ah affects one's Pilgrimage as a whole. During the tawaf, the pilgrim must feel the glory of the Holy Kaba'ah and its sacredness, in exactly the same way they feel for sala'at, or daily prayers, in order to raise their worship to a spiritual level. Throughout the tawaf, the pilgrim is supposed to clean through ablution. After completing the tawaf, the pilgrim proceeds to the Maqaam Ibrahim, the Station of Ibrahim, where they are required to offer two rak'ats of prayers. If a pilgrim is unable to pray there, because of lack of space, they can pray somewhere else.

Thereafter the pilgrim proceeds to the Zamzam well and, facing the Kaba'ah, partakes of the blessed water reciting:

> *"O My God, I pray to Thee for beneficial knowledge, abundant sustenance and to be cured of all diseases."*

The Sa'y

Then commences the Sa'y or the commemoration of Hagar's run between the hills of Safa and Marwah. The pilgrim emerges from the Bab al-Safa and ascends to the Mount Safa side, making his *niyat*, or intention, for the Sa'y. Keeping as clean as possible, the pilgrim faces the Kaba'ah, reciting the Qur'anic verse:

> *"The Safa and Marwah are truly amongst the signs of Allah."*

Then the pilgrims walk slowly or quickly to and fro, seven times, between the two points. The Sa'y can be performed while riding, though walking is still preferred. The aged and the handicapped are carried in litters.

The end of the Sa'y marks the end of the Umrah. The pilgrim can break the state of ihram by cutting the hair totally or partially. But this is only done on the day of *Nahr*, sacrifice.

Proceeding to Mina

At the end of the Sa'y, the pilgrim proceeds to Mina on the eighth day

Dhu al-Hijjah, or the day of *tarwiyah*. The pilgrim wears the ihram, choosing the state from one of the three kinds mentioned, and chants the talbiyah on the way. The pilgrim observes all the remaining prayers at Mina, spends the night there and, in keeping with the prophet's tradition, leaves the following day after sunrise.

Proceeding to Mount Arafat Wuqoof

Preparation for stopping at Arafat consists of bathing at Hamirah and reciting the talbiyah. The pilgrim then enters Arafat after sunset. The *wuqoof*, stopping at Mount Arafat, is considered the greatest part of the Pilgrimage. The Prophet Muhammad is remembered to have stated: "Hajj is Arafat". At Arafat, the pilgrim may sit, stand or lie down anywhere. There, at the bottom of a hill called the Mount of Mercy, the Prophet Muhammad delivered His farewell sermon. The wuqoof commemorates this event. The day of wuqoof is considered the one day on which God perfected Islam. It is an emotional day, when Muslims, clad in their common white ihram robes, gather from all corners of the world. Their hearts filled with devotion, the bare-headed masses cap this rocky mountain like one great canopy, seeking God's forgiveness, and affirming their faith in God through Islam. A number of prayers are recited here.

From Arafat to Muzdalifah

The pilgrims depart from Arafat only after sunset, in order to spend part of the day and night there. They then proceed to the lovely little town of Muzdalifah, about halfway between Mina and Arafat, chanting praises to God. On arrival, they perform the ablution. After the *adhan*, the call to prayer, they recite the *Maghrib* and *Isha'a* prayers and spend the night at Muzdalifah. The pilgrims are not allowed to leave before midnight. Though it is not compulsory, it is *sunnah,* traditional, to stay on until sunrise. After the morning prayers, visits may be made to monuments there. Before sunrise, the pilgrims proceed, tranquilly and solemnly, to *Wadi Muhassir*, through which they move at a quickened pace, on foot or

Left: Women do not have to wear the ihram, but they must cover their heads..

Below: Men must wear the ihram during the Pilgrimage.

Opposite: Pilgrims crowd around the slopes and peak of the Mount of Mercy.

in cars. The pilgrims pick up seven pebbles there, slightly "bigger than beans but smaller than peanuts". The pebbles may also be picked up at Mina.

Throwing Pebbles at the Aqaba Stone

On reaching the *jamratul* Aqaba, the Aqaba Stone, each pilgrim throws their set of seven pebbles, one at a time, at the Stone, one of three whitewashed, rectangular, masonry pillars, symbolising the stoning of the devils. The stoning is accompanied by uttering the talbiyah. The pilgrim starts throwing seven pebbles at the first *jamrah*, or pillar, next to the Khif mosque, keeping the mosque on his left and facing the Qiblah. They take a few steps, utter the right prayers, and go to the jamratul *wusta*, the middle jamrah, and throw pebbles at the largest pillar, representing Satan himself, who tried three times to persuade Ibrahim to disobey God's command to sacrifice his son.

Throwing the pebbles is symbolic of the pilgrim's redemption from evil. On the following days, the pilgrim throws 21 pebbles a day at the pillars. The pilgrims may nominate someone to throw the pebbles on their behalf if they have reasonable cause, such as a wounded arm, or old age.

At the end of the symbolic stoning, the pilgrims return to Mina, where they celebrate Idd-al-Adha, the Feast of Sacrifice, to mark the occasion. On this day, depending on their financial abilities, the pilgrims sacrifice sheep, goats, cows or other animals. The sacrifice symbolises Ibrahim's obedience in agreeing to sacrifice his son, or the sacrifice of what is dearest. It also means the renunciation of idolatrous sacrifice and is a way of offering thanks to God. It reinforces the Muslim ideal of sharing fortune with those who are less privileged. Muslims throughout the world perform the same rites on this day, spiritually in communion with the pilgrims in Mina. It is a bond of unity between them.

Release from the Ihram

The male pilgrim then cuts or trims his hair and women may cut a lock of their hair. With the completion of this ritual, the Muslim has virtually

fulfilled the greater part of his or her obligation as a pilgrim. The pilgrim then resumes normal life, except for sexual intercourse, or acts which may lead to it such as touching or kissing, which continue to be proscribed for a number of days.

Tawaf al-Ifadah

On returning to Makkah, the pilgrim performs a mandatory circling of the Kaba'ah seven times, known as tawaf *al-Ifadah*, as described before, to seal the Pilgrimage. The circling of the Kaba'ah this time is preferably done from midnight on the day of the sacrifice.

6. The Prophet's City: Madinah

The Brotherhood of Muslims — the Islamic religion — was born when the Prophet Muhammad was forced to leave Makkah and march 363 kilometres (227 miles) across the desert to the city of Madinah. At that time, at the start of the Hijrah, it was occupied by the tribes of Aus and Khazraj and a group of wealthy Jews.

None of those who accompanied the Prophet had anywhere to live and the first problem was to find housing. The Makkans were called Muhajirum and the Prophet told the people of Madinah: "Each Muhajir is your brother so it is your duty to help him". They responded so well that this came to be known, in turn, as *Ansaar*, which means, 'to help'.

Before this, however, the Prophet built a simple mud-and-wattle mosque at Quba, the spot where the Madinah people welcomed Him. He then remounted His camel and rode on. Everyone was anxious to receive Him as their guest and, to avoid appearing to favour any particular individual or family, the Prophet commanded His camel to ride forward and asked to be allowed to rest wherever the beast chose to stop. In an empty field, where it eventually stopped and knelt down, He dismounted and said: "Insha-Allah, this is our alighting place and final station." It was there that He built His own residence and the Mosque of the Prophet.

Pact with the Jews

After establishing the Islamic brotherhood, the Prophet set about bringing peace between the Muslims and the Jews so that each could live peacefully according to their beliefs. The agreement which He made between the Jews and His own people formed the constitution of Madinah. Some of its important sections provided for Jews and Muslims to unite to defend the city, for freedom of worship, a declaration of peace between the two, and that the Prophet act as the arbitrator in any dispute.

The first year in Madinah was one of settlement. But the Makkan infidels were set on destroying the Prophet and all He stood for. When

Previous pages: Pilgrims gather around to stone the pillars. Each stone must hit the mark.

they saw that more and more were joining Islam, they vowed to destroy the Muslims completely.

Battle of Badr AH2

When Muslims heard this, they planned to attack a Makkan caravan due to pass close to Madinah, but the leader came to learn of the Muslim plan and took another route, reaching Makkah safely. News of the planned ambush infuriated the Makkans and an army of more than a thousand was raised to march on Madinah in the month of Ramadhan. This was many months after the Prophet had settled in Madinah in the second year of the Hijrah.

The mighty army had a steed for each soldier, 700 camels and 300 horses. Compared with this force, the Prophet's army could only muster some 313 faithful. Nonetheless, they marched out to face the overwhelming odds and, when the battle at Badr started, Muhammad prayed aloud to Allah, which heartened all His men. Although outnumbered three-to-one, the Prophet's forces caused the Makkans to turn and flee, after killing their leader, Abu Jahl.

The Makkan infidels left behind 70 dead and 70 prisoners, while the Muslims mourned only 14. These, the first heroes of Islam, had entered Paradise.

Battle of Uhud AH3

Enraged, the Makkans vowed vengeance for their humiliating defeat. In Madinah, however, the victory reinforced Muhammad's influence. The most important result of the battle was the deepening of the faith of Muhammad Himself and His closest companions. After years of hardship and persecution, the astounding success was vindication of the faith which had sustained Him through disappointment. Inevitably, the Prophet was now committed to total war with the Makkan infidels.

The Makkans struck in March of 625CE, camping near Uhud. Almost at once, a scout brought exact information about their strength to Muhammad. A guard was kept over the Prophet's door all night and, early on Friday, after meeting with his generals, Muhammad ordered

Right: The voice of the Muezzin echoes from the minarets of the Prophet's Mosque, making the centuries-old call to prayer as the sun rises above the desert mountains.

Below: Families gather to pray in the Prophet's Mosque.

His men to confront the enemy before they razed the Madinah fields and crops. His army numbered 1,000 — much smaller again than the mighty force raised by the Makkan, which totalled 3,000. Even as He left the city, Muhammad suffered a terrible blow. Abdulla bin Bayy made some excuse and withdrew, leaving Muhammad with scarcely two-thirds of his original number.

They reached the mountain of Uhud, where the Prophet arranged His men in such a way that their backs were to the mountain, guarding their rear. But there was one pass through which infidels could strike. So Muhammad placed 50 archers there with orders not to move.

So resourceful were the Muslims that, after an initial thrust, the Makkans retreated, followed by the Muslim army. The archers posted to guard the pass, however, thought the battle had ended and, defying the Prophet's instruction, went to join their compatriots to celebrate.

When the Makkan commander, Khalid bin Walid, saw this, he went behind the mountain and came down the pass to attack the Muslims from the rear. In the confusion, many were slain and the Prophet Himself was injured and lost two teeth when a spear hit His face. But once again the Muslims found courage and drove back the Makkans in disarray, though losing 70 of their number, including the Prophet's uncle, Hazrat Hamza.

Uhud in Retrospect: Qur'anic Revelation

The Uhud debacle is mentioned in the Qur'an, wherein Allah rebukes the Muslims for failing to obey the Prophet. The hypocrites and the Jews, however, rejoiced and began to plot against the Muslims.

The Siege: Battle of Khanaq AH5

The Battle of Uhud was inconclusive, neither an overwhelming defeat for the Muslims nor an unqualified victory for the Makkans. On this they brooded and, during the next two years, the Makkans raised a powerful confederate army, numbering 10,000 men, made up of two, perhaps three armies: one of the Quraysh and their allies of around 4,000 men,

Ghatafan leading a second and Sulaym with a third.

To oppose this enormous force, the most Muhammad could count on was 3,000 people — virtually the entire population of Madinah, save for the Jewish tribe of the Quraysh, which seems to have wished to stay neutral.

The enemy approached the city by wadi al-Aqiq and some camped there and some at Uhud, but then they found themselves checked. As soon as Muhammad heard news of their advance from Makkah, He called His advisers and they devised a means of defence previously unheard-of in Arabia.

For six days and nights, the Muslims laboured to dig a wide, dry moat, a trench, wherever Madinah lay open to cavalry attack. The 600 horses of the Makkans proved of no advantage. For weeks, the besieged citizens withstood the repeated forays of the enemy and repelled them. Those who attempted to cross the trench were cut to pieces. The trench, which was three metres deep, three metres wide and several kilometres long, was impassable. At the end of the siege, the temperature dropped suddenly and a fierce wind that arose destroyed the tents of the Makkan so badly that they were left in disarray and had to retreat.

Treaty of Hudaybiya AH6

As a result of a dream, Muhammad assembled 1,400 faithful Muslims, including the nomads of Khuza'ah, to make Umrah to Makkah. As He approached the Holy City, the Makkans became fearful and sent out 200 cavalry to meet Him and bar the way. But Muhammad foiled them by taking an unusual route through hilly and difficult country to reach Al-Hudaybiya at the edge of the sacred territory. There His camel refused to go further so He halted.

The Makkans threatened Muhammad and warned they would fight if He tried to perform the Pilgrimage. After many exchanges of messages and discussions, a treaty was agreed upon. The gist of it was that, subject to the Muslims returning to Madinah and making the Pilgrimage the following year, the Makkans would evacuate the city for three days. One aspect of these talks was a pledge made by Muhammad's Muslim

Above: The carvings that crown one of the earliest gates of the Mosque.

Below: The craftmanship of the Islamic masons and sculptors is revealed in this entrance to the Mosque.

supporters when it looked as if the talks would break down.

This was the Pledge of Good Pleasure, or the Pledge Under the Tree.

   The treaty stipulated that:

(a)   the Muslims would return to Madinah;

(b)   they would make the Pilgrimage the following year and would be allowed three days in Makkah;

(c)   they should carry no arms but swords;

(d)   there would be peace between Muslims and Makkans for 10 years;

(e)   any tribe of Arabia was to join either of the parties to the treaty so long as they were also bound by the treaty.

   On conclusion of the treaty, Muhammad slaughtered His sacrificial animal and shaved His hair, and the others followed His example.

Battle of Khaybar AH7

The Jews of Madinah were rich and powerful but, as Islam grew stronger, they began plotting against the Muslims. These secret plans became known and two Jewish tribes were expelled from the city. They moved about 130 kilometres from Madinah, to a place called Khaybar whence they despatched agents throughout Arabia to incite the infidels against the Muslims, gathering an army of 24,000 to march on Muhammad and His companions.

   On hearing this, the Prophet brought His armies to battle readiness and set out on a march to the Jewish stronghold. After a long and tempestuous struggle, with many battles, the Jews were vanquished and, when the Muslims occupied their fortresses, pleaded for mercy. A peace treaty was signed and the Jews gave no more trouble.

Conquest of Makkah AH8

One of the clauses of the peace treaty between Muslims and Makkans was that friends of either party would not fight the other. But on the 10th of Ramadhan, AH8, Banu Khuza'ah, a tribe friendly with the Muslims, was attacked by Banu Bakr, a tribe friendly with the Makkans.

   Muhammad then marched to the Holy City with 10,000 men, and

when this mighty force arrived at the city gates, the Makkans were so greatly afraid that they surrendered at once. The next day, Muhammad led His men into the city. The rule of the infidels had ended. Entering the Kaba'ah, the Prophet destroyed all the idols and, after prayers, pardoned all His former enemies with the words, "May Allah forgive you".

Farewell Pilgrimage AH10

After the conquest of Makkah through surrender, there was peace throughout the land and the Prophet invited all to join Him for the Pilgrimage in the 10th year of the Hijrah.

Thousands flocked to Madinah where, on the 26th day of the Dhu al-Qa'dah, after Zuhr prayers, the Prophet set out on His farewell Pilgrimage, stopping 10 kilometres from the city at a place called Hulaifah to spend the night. Next morning, He donned the cloth of the Pilgrimage, the ihram, mounted His camel and began to call out, "Labbaik, Allahumma! Labbaik!", to be joined by thousands in His wake.

He reached Makkah on the fifth day of Dhu al-Hijjah, travelling the following morning to Arafat, where He prayed all day before delivering His final message to the vast throng of Muslims gathered there with Him, more than 100,000:

> "O people, listen carefully for perhaps I may not meet you again at this place.
> "From today all interest is unlawful. First of all I will not take interest which my uncle Abbas is to pay me.
> "There will be no blood feuds from now on. To begin with, I forgive the murderers of my nephew Rabia.
> "Be kind to your women as it is your duty to look after them.
> "Be kind to your slaves and give them the best food and clothes.
> "All Muslims are brothers. All men are equal. Birth, colour or race does not make a person better than another.
> "Remember, the life, honour and property of a brother Muslim should be more sacred to you than this day, this month and this place.

Opposite: Minaret of the Prophet's Mosque stands with elegance against the sky.

Right: The craftmanship of many architectural eras graces the inner court of the Prophet's Mosque where Muslims pray.

> "I am leaving behind two things, the Qur'an and my Sunnah.
> "If you hold fast to them you will never go astray."

After a long pause, He asked the throng: "Have I delivered my message to you?"

Came thousands of voices in reply: "Yes, it is so."

Then the Prophet raised His eyes to the sky and said: "Allah, you are my witness".

Shortly afterwards, the following verses of the Qur'an were revealed:

> "Today I have perfected your faith and completed my blessing
> on you and chosen Islam as your religion".

This was the first and last Hajj of the Prophet.

Prophet's Illness and Death AH10

After the farewell Pilgrimage, the Prophet returned to Madinah, where He had only 80 days left to live.

He was taken ill with high fever but went about His daily prayers and leadership until He became too weak to go to the Mosque. Abu Bakr led the prayers in his place.

On the morning of Monday, the 12th day of Rabi-ul-Awwal, the Prophet appeared to recover but at mid-day He relapsed and died.

He was buried the following day and today His tomb is a revered shrine.

The Succession

Upon His death, the news spread quickly and stunned crowds gathered in the Prophet's Mosque. A loyal friend, Umar, drew his sword and said: "If anyone says the Prophet is dead, I will cut his head off." But when Abu Bakr appeared and the people questioned him, he called out: "O people, if anyone among you worshipped Muhammad, let him know that He is dead. But if you worshipped Allah, then He is living and will never die."

And when it came to choosing a successor to the Prophet, two who were nominated refused, saying it should only be Abu Bakr, the companion who had joined the Prophet on the Hijrah, and, by general agreement, he became first Caliph of Islam.

Madinah — After the Hajj

Although a visit to Madinah does not constitute a mandatory part of the Pilgrimage, few who perform the Hajj miss the opportunity to visit the city and its many historic sites. These include:

Mosque of Al-Azhab

The Mosque of al-Azhab is on the site of the defensive trench built during the great siege.

Mosque of the Al-Quba

A simple whitewashed mosque, known as the al-Quba, stands on the spot where the Prophet was welcomed to Madinah and where He built the city's — and Islam's — first mosque, a simple building of mud and wattle. Two sala'ats, unity prayers, said in this Mosque are equal to a Lesser Pilgrimage, for Muhammad Himself said:

> *"He who purifies himself at home, then comes to the Mosque of Quba and performs a prayer, his prayer will be equal to a Lesser Pilgrimage."*

Mosque of the Prophet

After completing this monument to Allah, Muhammad remounted his camel and rode off into Madinah, where his camel stopped in the empty field and knelt, and the Prophet said: "Insha-Allah, this is our alighting place and our final station."

Above the Mosque of the Prophet now stands a green dome. It was

Left: One of the early gates of the Prophet's Mosque.

Opposite: Noonday crowds wander through the streets outside the Prophet's Mosque.

Below: The interior of the Prophet's Mosque. The arcades in the foreground are modern, and those in the background are from the Ottoman period.

there that the Prophet died in 632CE, aged 62. Muslims believe a prayer in this Mosque is worth a thousand prayers elsewhere, except those made at the Sacred Mosque in Mecca.

The pilgrim enters the Mosque with his right foot first, saying:

> *"In the name of Allah, and may the blessing and peace of God be upon His Messenger. O Allah, grant Your blessing to Muhammad and to his family, and forgive me and open for me the doors of Your mercy."*

He then prays, performing two prostrations as a greeting to the Mosque. Now he faces the grave, turning his back to the Qiblah, and says:

> *"Peace be upon You, O Messenger of Allah, peace be upon You, O Prophet of Allah, peace be upon You, O most exalted of Allah's creatures, peace be upon You, Messenger of Allah who is Lord of the world."*

Two dark-green silk shrouds cover two other tombs in the Prophet's Mosque: that of his close friend, Abu Bakr, which is to the right of the Prophet's tomb and, next to that, the grave of the Commander of the Faithful, Omar ibn al-Khattab.

The pilgrim must pray before both these graves. Once these dedications have been completed, he bows in prayer for his family, his friends, his Muslim brothers and himself.

To the pilgrim, the Mosque is alive with faith and everything in which a Muslim believes, for it is there that the virtues of goodness, brotherhood, unselfishness and love first blossomed.

There are many other monuments in Madinah, great shrines such as the Mosque of al-Jumaa, where the Prophet offered up Islam's first Friday prayer.

Mosque of al-Ghamamah

There is also the Mosque of al-Ghamamah, which was a favourite prayer place of the Prophet, and also the Mosque of the Qiblatain, which is of immense importance in Islamic history.

It was there that the Prophet revealed the Surah commanding all Muslims to face towards Makkah — and the Kaba'ah — in prayer, and not towards Jerusalem. The Qiblah that used to face Jerusalem still stands. But in other mosques, those facing Jerusalem have been walled up.

In Madinah are also the graves of such martyrs as Hazrat Hamza, Lion of Allah and the Lion of His Messenger. The city is also home to the Islamic University and Qur'anic Library.

Thus, for many pilgrims, a visit to Madinah and the Mosque of the Prophet is the only way to end the Pilgrimage, bearing in mind Muhammad's words:

> *"One prayer in my Mosque is better than a thousand, except in the Holy Mosque of Makkah."*

Left: Glittering chandeliers light the corridor which leads to the doors of the Prophet's Tomb, adorned with beautiful carvings of wrought metal and wood.

Below: Deep inside the Mosque, close to the Prophet's Tomb, lights gleam on the delicate carving of the Imam's mihbar, or pulpit.

7. Modern Makkah

As a city which depends heavily on revenue from pilgrims, who have numbered up to three million during recent Pilgrimages, modern Makkah has adapted well to the changing needs of visitors.

Today, the city is a modern one with a resident population of about 400,000 provided with most of the facilities that have become the basic essentials of the modern city.

Makkah's streets are crammed with cars, pick-ups, limousines, minibuses and buses. Its handful of luxury hotels are air-conditioned, catering for wealthy Muslim visitors.

Though the King of Saudi Arabia is resident in Riyadh, the seat of government is still in Makkah, the original capital of Arabia and a city which has continued to exert its influence in international affairs.

A number of service ministries have come into existence to cater specifically for the welfare of the pilgrims: ministries of the interior, Pilgrimage, public health and communications; other departments, such as security, traffic control and passports, along with the ports and airport authorities, supplement the services of the ministries for the pilgrims. Millions of Saudi riyals are spent annually by Saudi Arabia to improve the infrastructure in order to meet the ever-increasing demands upon it.

The discovery of oil in the Saudi Kingdom has had a big impact on the growth and development of Makkah. The area of the city today is 71 square kilometres. Four fountains now cool the view of the city in four main squares. Contrary to the past, the buildings surrounding the Haram Mosque now tower to some 13 storeys, with adequate adjoining space and streets.

Accommodation facilities in Makkah fluctuate between two extremes. The city is almost over-utilised during the Pilgrimage, posing a serious problem.

However, Pilgrimage accommodation is not restricted to the city centre alone; it is spread to the outlying quarters, such as Al-Azizyya, Al-Nuzha, Al-Zahir and Al-Zuhara. Still, accommodating millions of pilgrims in a small city within such a short period is an enormous task in terms of organisation. Accommodation is greatly aided by the *mutawwafs*, or traditional pilgrim guides, who offer group

accommodation for the pilgrims and oversee their local transportation.

The well-to-do pilgrims are better off because they can afford hotel accommodation or can rent private, modern apartments in Makkah and Madinah. Such accommodation is usually booked in advance through agents.

The local taxi is the common mode of transport in Makkah, but now there are scheduled coach services between Jeddah and Makkah and Jeddah and Madinah, at fixed rates. Pilgrims usually land in Jeddah by air or sea and after completing immigration and customs formalities proceed to Makkah. Jeddah, Makkah and Madinah are linked by modern motorways that allow fast movement. In order to reduce the build-up of traffic around the Holy Mosque, a new tunnel for vehicles was constructed.

In 1988CE (1408AH), King Fahd laid the foundation stone for the third Saudi expansion of the Holy Mosques of Makkah and Madinah.

The new development of the Holy Mosque in Makkah includes expansion of the western wing,, which now holds more than a million worshippers during the Holy months. There are 60,000 square metres of prayer area covering the enlarged roof in addition to 86,000 square metres covering the surrounding plaza. Two towering minarets have been added to the previous seven. A new entrance and 18 other gates have also been built.

New prayer halls on the ground and first floors are complete with tiles made of heat-resistant marble and the whole structure is now cooled by one of the world's largest air-conditioning units. To facilitate movement during the Hajj, escalators have been added alongside the stairs on the northern and southern sides of the building. Other improvements include a new drainage system.

Expansion work on the Prophet's Mosque was begun in 1985CE (1405AH) and the Mosque can now accommodate more than a million worshippers. The work included 27 main plazas, each capped with a state-of-the-art sliding dome that can be opened or closed according to the weather, and six additional minarets, each with a four-ton gold-plated crescent. Seven newly constructed entrances ensure the smooth passage of pilgrims. The new extensions have been fitted with a suitable

number of staircases and escalators. There is additional roof area for praying, and 12 huge mechanically operated Teflon umbrellas have been constructed to protect pilgrims from the sun and high temperatures.

The vast basement complex is constructed to include the service equipment and wiring needs, as well as other maintenance infrastructure.

The decoration and architectural finishing matches the earlier building work and features exquisitely crafted pillars, cornices, golden grilles, brass doors and marble work.

Glossary of terms

Ablution: Purifying oneself with water before offering prayers, reading the holy Qur'an, performing the Hajj, Umrah or any kind of worship of Allah

Adhan: The call to prayer, recited loudly to announce that the time for prayer is due

AH: After the Hijrah

Allah: The principal Muslim name for God

Allah-u-Akbar: Allah is great

Ansaar: To help

Arafat: Name of the mountain and adjacent plain where pilgrims spend the ninth day of Dhu al-Hijjah

Bait: House

Bait-al-atiq: The Ancient House

Baytullah: The House of God

Bedouin: The traditional desert people of Saudi Arabia

Caliph: Successors of the Prophet Muhammad as rulers of the Islamic world

CE: Christian Era

Dhu al-Hijjah: Twelfth month of the Muslim calender

Fidya: Compensation offered for breaking any of the Muslim rules

Haram: Mosque (Masjid)

Hajj: The Pilgrimage to Mecca

Hadith: The traditions of the Prophet — His deeds and sayings

Hijrah: Migration of the Prophet Muhammad to Mecca

Imam: Person who leads others in prayers

Ihram: The pilgrim's robe — two lengths of seamless linen, towels or sheets, usually white, worn during Umrah or Hajj

Isha'a: Night Prayer, which begins about one-and-a-half hours after sunset

Jamrah: Three places between Muzdalifah and Mina depicting the point of stoning the devil

Jamratul: One of the three stones (pillars) situated in Mina. One of the ceremonies of the Pilgrimage is to throw pebbles at these stones, which stand as symbols of Satan

Kaba'ah: A black cube-shaped stone edifice towards which all Muslims turn their faces in prayer

Kadhi: Muslim Chief Judge

Khutba: Friday sermon

Kiswah: Cloth covering for the Kaba'ah

Madhhab: School of Islamic law

Maghrib: Sunset Prayer

Majlis: Family groups

Maqaam Ibrahim: The place where the Prophet Ibrahim stood while he and Ismael were building the Kaba'ah

Marwah: Hill near the Kaba'ah

Masa: Subway-like lane between the two hills Safa and Marwah

Masjid: The Mosque, place of prostration

Mataf: Area of circumambulation round the Kaba'ah

Mihrab: The niche in a Mosque showing the direction of Mecca

Mina: A place outside Mecca on the road to Arafat

Miqat: Boundary of the area around Makkah, before entering which a pilgrim has to be in ihram

Mu'tameer: One intending to perform Umrah

Mutawwaf: Pilgrim guide, who offers group accomodation and oversees local transportation

Muzdalifah: Valley between Arafat and Mina, where pilgrims returning from Arafat spend a night

Myzab: Water spout which drains rainwater away from the roof of the Kaba'ah

Nahr: Day of sacrifice

Nadi gawn: Town forum in the square of Kaba'ah

Nashsh: Business, enterprise

Niyat: Intention of doing something

Qiblah: Direction of the Kaba'ah in Mecca from where one is standing; the direction of prayer

Qur'an: Final revealed Scriptures given by God to Muhammad

Rak'at: Muslim prayers consist of Rak'at, which comprises one bowing and two prostrations

Ramadhan: The month of fasting. In this month, the Holy Qur'an began to be revealed to the Prophet Muhammad

Safa: Mountain near the Kaba'ah

Sa'y: The cermony of walking and partly running seven times between Safa and Marwah, performed during the Hajj or Umrah

Sala'at: Prayer, as an act of piety

Shahada: Faith

Sharif: A descendant of the Prophet Muhammad; one who has inherited spiritual power

Sunnah: The traditions and practices of the Prophet, which became models for all Muslims to follow

Surah: A chapter division of the Qur'an

Tajir: Businessman

Talbiyah: Incantation for the pilgrims, chanted loudly by male pilgrims but only loudly enough to be heard by her neighbour by the female pilgrim, saying "Laibaik, Allahumma! Laibaik!"

Tarwiya: Eighth day of Dhu al-Hijjah, when pilgrims start going to Mina

Tawaf: Circumambulation — circling the Kaba'ah anti-clockwise seven times, beginning and ending at the Black Stone

Tawaf-al-Hadah: Circling the Kaba'ah seven times on returning to Makkah, to seal the Pilgrimage. Preferably done from midnight on the day of the sacrifice

Umm al Qura: The mother of cities

Umrah: Lesser Pilgrimage of Bait-Allah during the year, any time other than the month of Hajj. Two Umrahs are said to be equal to one Hajj

Wazzan: Professional weighers

Wuqoof: Staying in Arafat any time between sunrise and sunset on the ninth day of Dhu al-Hijjah. The day of Wuqoof is considered the one day on which God perfected Islam

Zakat: Alms — a certain fixed portion of the wealth of each Muslim to be paid for the benefit of the needy. Obligatory to all Muslims

Zamzam: Sacred well inside the Haram Mosque. Its water is pure and blessed

Zamzamis: Those who provide water for Muslims

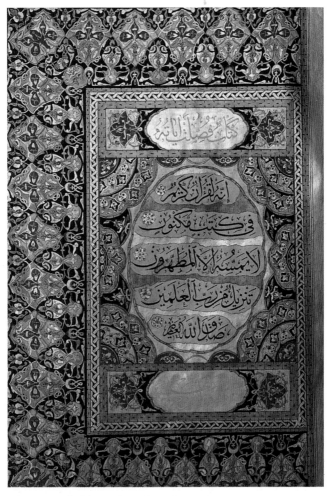

Above: Detail of a page from the early Qur'an.
Previous page:s: Thousands of people gather around the Kaba'ah for the evening prayers.